...om many written for the comfort
...ind of un-intrusive compassion, an
...ver the really hard questions. The
scholar...p ...g experience, serve to enhance the
gift of what I can but call *courtesy*: respect for the strangeness of
grief, a gift to be accepted in whatever way and degree it is needed."

Rosemary Luling Haughton
Wellspring House

"Death is not an easy topic to address. Yet, Fr. Nolan shows no fear
in speaking directly to and about this mystery, as well as gathering
the wisdom of great poets and thinkers who also share a vision of
hope. A fine volume for all pastoral ministers."

†Robert F. Morneau
Auxiliary Bishop of Green Bay

"The fruit of many years of prayer, reading, and preaching on death,
dying, and life after death, I value this practical collection for its
brief, insightful meditations and for its suggested prayers that may
be incorporated into the Funeral Liturgy and Burial Rite."

Fr. William Bergen, S.J.
Church of St. Ignatius Loyola, New York City

"No sentimental, saccharin musings here, rather, wisdom from
down the centuries and across human cultures in a respectfully ecu-
menical style. It will be immensely useful to those whose grief at
the loss of a loved one, or whose fear of their own inevitable death,
is made the more painful by skepticism concerning a promised
afterlife. Fr. Nolan's wholesome attitude toward the mystery of
death will awaken in readers a peaceful anticipation of the journey
from life to Life."

Father Richard G. Rento, STL
Diocese of Paterson

"*They Shall Be Comforted* is a book for those concerned with death,
a recent death of a relative or friend, or one's own impending death.
A pastor will want to keep this book handy, not only for his personal meditation or contemplation, but also for his counsel to those
who are finding death a heavy cross. I think, as well, a person finding the prospect of death very difficult may benefit in spending
time with this book."

†William A. Hughes
Bishop Emeritus of Covington

Twenty-Third Publications
185 Willow Street
P.O. Box 180
Mystic, CT 06355
(860) 536-2611
(800) 321-0411

ISBN: 0-89622-978-5
Library of Congress Catalog Card Number: 99-70801
Printed in the U.S.A.

CONTENTS

INTRODUCTION

Few people think about death, and many have trouble believing in resurrection. I offer these words to the living, for meditation, prayer, and consolation, because they are true. They reflect the truth of what a Christian believes of Jesus Christ and God's word. These subjects call for a language that not only communicates but brings us into communion with Truth. We do not need mystifying words to speak of the great Mysteries, but we do need poetry, the language of metaphor. We need something easier to grasp than the writing of many theologians.

For instance, there is the valuable book, *A History of Heaven*, by Jeffrey Burton Russell (Princeton University Press, 1997). It is really not a history but a profound meditation on what the teachers of the church, the mystics, and the poet Dante have said about eternal life. For those who can stay with scholarship, it is profoundly satisfying, even exciting. Another author, Caroline Walker Bynum, wrote *The Resurrection of the Body in Western Christianity 200-1336* (Columbia University Press, 1995). This, too, is helpful to those who can take it. This present book, or collection, seeks to fulfill a pastoral or popular need, and is indebted to scholars like these. And many others.

People have thought about death but often in fearful ways. I wish to go beyond this; some of the words that follow, not all mine, should move us like great music. Some would say it all comes down to faith, but faith is illumined by words. For instance, after finishing this manuscript, I found this couplet by the seventeenth-century German mystic Angelus Silesius:

> Love like a magnet is, it draws me into God,
> And what is greater still, it pulls God into death.

"Love pulls God into death." Is the mystic saying that God's grace will suffice in the time of our passion? Yes, but more. Is he not also saying that God enters the passion of our lives in the Incarnation, confronts it in the person of Jesus, and gives us hope? Yes, but still more. When people find it difficult to believe in God, the starting point is often creation. Cosmic power is everywhere; the usual name we give to this power is God. When creation becomes conscious—in us, in the human—we ask the deepest question: is this power a personal love? The whole story of Israel and Jesus affirms that it is. But then another question, which Angelus Silesius answers: can this power we know as love overcome "the last of the evils which is death"? The resurrection of Jesus, and his presence in us, is the answer.

We all need to think of these things, not only because we are mortal, but because death usually comes unexpectedly and we need to say goodbye to those we have loved with proper rituals and the right words. People who have been part of our lives should be remembered with gratitude. And, for believers, faith should be strengthened. It's also true that time hangs heavily upon those who wait upon death (God's moment), in a hospital or hospice, or at home. It is a time when we can pray, read parts of the Bible (especially some of the psalms), and perhaps some of the prayers and reflections in this book. The lovely words of St. Augustine ("Watch thou, dear Lord, with those who wake, or watch, or weep tonight, and give thine angels and saints charge over those who sleep") best express what I mean. The oft-quoted words of Cardinal Newman (page 114), help us to have faith when life itself seems senseless or at least without direction. The Prayer of Commendation (page 126) breathes a confident hope, and may be recited when someone is about to leave us for God. Many of the reflections are from my Easter sermons or funeral homilies or lectures on the resurrection.

Much of this book is addressed to believers in the Christian faith—Catholic, Protestant, Orthodox. But "death is the unexceptional sentence passed on everyone," and I hope that other believers, humanists, and those who arrange secular memorials may also find passages that will be helpful. Whatever our approach to death—and to God—we are right to treat the moment with dignity, and to appreciate, even to celebrate, the gift of a person's life.

Rev. Joseph T. Nolan
Boston College
August 15, 1998

REFLECTIONS

ETERNAL LIFE

Eternal life begins now; its climax is heaven. Heaven as a word has become too familiar to us, almost shopworn. It is in use every day, sometimes just as an exclamation or a substitute for God's name, as when we say in exasperation, "What in heaven's name are you doing?" What image do you have of heaven? Some images have hardly filled us with longing! Much as we esteem a choir, we don't want to be part of a perpetual sing-along. And even though we dress in white occasionally, we want a bigger wardrobe than white robes and palms. Yes, these images come from the Bible. But the word "images" gives us a clue: they also come from the imagination. This is really a wonderful power; we use it to "get a handle" on an invisible reality. But what is that? Heaven? Paradise? Eternal life? These are still words. Even "God" is a word for ultimate reality. We speak and think and dream out of our limitations as human beings; perhaps St. Paul put it best when he said, "I see now as in a glass, darkly; then I shall see face to face. Now I have only glimpses of knowledge, but then I shall know, even as I am known" (1 Corinthians 13:12).

The gospels give other images of heaven. One is a mansion with many rooms. That may appeal to some; to others it might suggest a reservation in a comfortable inn! There is also the simple reference of Jesus to his Father. He invites us to come to the Father—with him (and through him). For many—perhaps all—of us, that should be enough. Surely the word "Father" suggests life as well as power, and trust. And the very word *Jesus* has come to mean love and forgiveness. Companion, friend. Lover, brother, bridegroom. All these are precious words or images; they tell us much about God.

When a theologian uses the term "beatific vision" for heaven, it may help, but it may also send us back to the poets. With them, as with all true artists, God has "put his eye into their hearts." They are enabled to see the world as a sacrament, revealing the divine. They sense that it is "an intimation of immortality." They are enabled to reflect on human experience and feel that it is a clue to the joy of a life fulfilled—but not yet. This is the way Thomas Wolfe spoke of something that happens every day—dying, and going to heaven:

To lose the earth you have
for greater knowing,
to lose the life you have
for greater love,
to leave the friends you loved
for greater loving,
to find a land more kind than home.

Note how familiar are the references—earth, life, love, friends, and home. We know these, we enjoy them. He is saying we have not lost them. All that we have known and loved, and we ourselves, are transformed by the creative power of God. It is this loving power that first made and now remakes us. What Jesus said of himself could be said of each of us: "The Father lives in me, accomplishing his works." On earth that work is bringing about the kingdom. Beyond earth it is to bring us to the fullness of life in God.

JESUS CALMS A STORM

Luke 8:22–25

One day he got into a boat with his disciples, and he said to them, "Let us go across to the other side of the lake." So they put out, and while they were sailing he fell asleep. A windstorm swept down on the lake, and the boat was filling with water, and they were in danger. They went to him and woke him up, shouting, "Master, Master, we are perishing!" And he woke up and rebuked the wind and the raging waves; they ceased, and there was a calm. He said to them, "Where is your faith?" They were afraid and amazed, and said to one another, "Who then is this, that he commands even the winds and the water, and they obey him?"

POWER OVER DEATH

We are perhaps familiar with the gospel image of Jesus calming the storm at sea (Luke 8:22–25). The sea is a symbol or the image of the tides of death which threaten us, roll over us, and finally break down the small, frail craft which is the vessel of our body seeking to protect us against the onslaught. How the body fights to live! God made us for life, and the body has marvelous powers to fight off infection, illness, and the threat of dying. We struggle for breath—for life—in our first moments and in our last. But at one point the battle is lost, and literature is full of the theme of death as conqueror.

They have it wrong. Christ is conqueror. That is the deepest meaning of the gospel (and of being a Christian). We are told of the divine power over nature in the book of Job. We hear that power described in the gospel: "Who can this one be, that the wind and the sea obey him?" But there is no reason, if we know the whole story of Jesus, to think that his power over nature does not include human nature, with its built-in mortality. He has the power not merely to rescue us at sea but to rescue us from the storms of life and the abyss of nonexistence.

How do people, be they believers or unbelievers, face death? In many ways. Here are some of the thoughts they recorded. The first is from Cicero, the Roman statesman who lived just before Jesus, dying in 44 B.C. Cicero wrote, "I look forward to my dissolution as to a secure haven, where I shall at length find a happy repose from the fatigues of a long journey" (*Essay on Old Age*). It is a pleasing statement and yet it might strike someone as no more than a dreamless sleep. Here are two other views on death and dying from the people we used to call pagans. This is from the slave philosopher Epictetus, who lived at the same time as Jesus:

> Remind thyself that he whom thou lovest is
> mortal—that what thou lovest is not thine own;
> it is given thee for the present, not irrevocably
> nor forever, but even as a fig or a bunch of
> grapes at the appointed season of the year . . . .

This view suggests that death is part of nature and comes in due season. It reminds us of the wise man who wrote in Greek for the Hebrew tradition: "For everything there is a time." The Roman does not write with a sense of fatalism nor is this the Stoic idea of accepting the inevitable with good grace. The beautiful phrase, "What thou lovest is not thine own," suggests that each of us belongs to Another who at some point calls us home. Life and the beloved "is given thee for the present," he declares. Who is the Giver? Is it not the One who ripens the grapes and spins the planets and rejoices to let us share existence, who gives us the promise of fuller, richer life than we now enjoy?

11

Another statement by Epictetus reinforces this view:

> "Never say about anything, 'I have lost it,' but only 'I have given it back.' Is your child dead? It has been given back. Is your wife dead? She has been returned" (*Discourses*).

How could pagan philosophers come this close to the truth? They did not have revelation. No, but it is quite possible they had faith—and that kind of inspiration which comes from the Spirit. We are told that the Spirit blows, or moves, where it wills, and that reminds us that the truths we hold are often reinforced for us when we discover that others in different cultures or traditions believe the same. Belief in immortality, not just the hope of it, is as old as religion, and some would say as old as humans.

It is easier for us to believe because of Jesus. His story is engraved on our hearts. And everywhere, in our churches and in our homes, we put up the sign of his death, the cross or the crucifix, because it has also become for us a sign of life. It signifies his surrender to that Love which is stronger than death. St. Paul reminds us of Christianity's most basic truth, that "Christ for our sake has died and has been raised up." We hold this on faith. Jesus appeals to the faith of the disciples when they ask him to rescue them. He will not always deliver us as we wish when danger threatens; prayer is no insurance policy against accident, illness, or dying. But he will deliver us to peace of mind and from eternal death, from dissolution and darkness. He is the light that came into the world, and this light cannot be swallowed up in the darkness. Then why are we terrified sometimes at what tomorrow brings, or the thought of dying? We have many reasons to stand in wonder and amazement at this one whom the winds and the sea obey.

THE TRANSFIGURATION

Mark 9: 2–8

Six days later, Jesus took with him Peter and James and John, and led them up a high mountain apart, by themselves. And he was transfigured before them, and his clothes became dazzling white, such as no one on earth could bleach them. And there appeared to them Elijah with Moses, who were talking with Jesus. Then Peter said to Jesus, "Rabbi, it is good for us to be here; let us make three dwellings, one for you, one for Moses, and one for Elijah." He did not know what to say, for they were terrified. Then a cloud overshadowed them, and from the cloud there came a voice, "This is my Son, the Beloved; listen to him!" Suddenly when they looked around, they saw no one with them any more, but only Jesus.

MEANING TO SUFFERING?

In the gospels we read of the Transfiguration, Jesus caught up in glory on the mountain. Just before this scene is told in Mark's gospel, Jesus had predicted his own suffering and drew a horrified reaction from his followers. They reject the very thought.

What is going on here? What is the connection between this prediction and the Transfiguration scene? This: the Hebrews had slowly built up an awareness of the messiah to come as a suffering servant; it begins with passages in Isaiah. The Hebrew feast of tabernacles centered around the enthronement of a suffering messiah clothed in white. So the Transfiguration gospel is written with that in mind; the Jewish listeners would recognize it and be encouraged to take hope, to look beyond the passion to what we now call the resurrection.

But the apostles remain puzzled. And so do we, at the existence of pain and suffering. How about these answers: they come from the great short-story writer Isaac Bashevis Singer, or really, from his father, when the son asked him to explain the mystery of suffering. His father made several tries:

First, he said, it simply goes with having a body. Body and pain are inevitable; they are synonymous.

His second try: some suffering (not all, but a lot of it), comes from the abuse of freedom, free will.

Third, his father referred to God's infinite goodness and his plans for us, implying that all this is greater than the pain.

But finally he cut short the conversation by reminding his son that it was time to go to the synagogue and say the afternoon prayer.

It is not likely that the father was just tired of talking—rather, he recognizes that before the mystery of pain one can, in the end, only pray and seek an answer in faith. And what we discover is that the mystery of God—or love—is greater. God, in a sense, confronts us and says, "Will you trust me?" And, like Job, we surrender.

WHAT IS IT THAT I LOVE?

What is it that I love, when I love my God?
Not the beauty of any body,
nor the splendor of time.
Not the radiance of the light, so pleasing to our eyes.
Not the sweet melodies of songs of all kinds,
nor the fragrance of flowers and ointments and spices;
not manna and honey,
nor limbs delightful to the embrace of flesh and blood.
Not these things do I love when I love my God.

And yet do I love a kind of light,
a kind of sound, a kind of fragrance and food;
a kind of embracing,
in loving my God who is the light,
who is the sound, and the fragrance,
who is the food, and the embracing of my inner self—

where the light shines into my soul
which no place can hold,
where that music sounds which time
cannot snatch away,
where that fragrance comes which no breeze disperses,
where that food is taken which no eating can diminish,
and that embrace is given which no satiety can sunder.
All this is what I love when I love my God.

St. Augustine

DYING IS GOOD NIGHT

Words are difficult at a time like this, but words can help, because they remind us of what our faith teaches, and what we, in our heart of hearts, believe. The words that follow are a meditation on God's love.

When we were little children, perhaps we went to sleep to the sound of a lullaby. We may not even remember them, but they helped us to feel secure, that all was right with the world. Lullabies breathe the gentle, providential love which parents feel for their child. And they give us a precious clue, a hint, of God's love for us. Few songs have better expressed this than the words as well as the lovely music of the Welsh folk song, "All Through the Night."

> Sleep, my child, and peace attend thee
> all through the night;
> guardian angels God will send thee
> all through the night;
> soft the drowsy hours are creeping,
> hill and vale in slumber steeping,
> I my loving vigil keeping,
> all through the night.

It is God who keeps vigil, day and night, through our living and our dying, through our rejoicing and our sorrowing. It is God whose love would cradle us, sustain us. Here is the other stanza of the hymn:

While the moon her watch is keeping,
all through the night;
while the weary world is sleeping,
all through the night;
o'er thy spirit gently stealing,
visions of delight revealing,
breathes a pure and holy feeling,
all through the night.

As much as words can do, these suggest the presence of God at the core of our being. "Breathes a pure and holy feeling," writes the poet. That feeling is more like a longing for one who is already there: God who is hidden all through our lives, glimpsed only now and then, the one who holds out, in the future he has promised us, "visions of delight."

A beautiful poem. But still more beautiful because, in God, it is true.

THE PASSION—
OF JESUS, AND OURS

Jesus was a Jew, dying at the hands of the leaders of his people and the indifferent Romans. Everything he had dared and preached and stood for seemed to crumble that Thursday night as even his friends fled into the darkness— all but one, the one he had called the rock, and Peter was now frantically claiming that he had never known him. In this awful situation did Jesus begin to doubt or deny God? All we know from the passion account is that he continued to pray to him, even though it says his heart was nearly broken with sorrow, and his sweat became as drops of blood falling to the ground.

Jesus had lived his life with an astonishing awareness, even intimacy, with the one that he called Abba, Father. Scholars argue over which words he actually spoke. They have written volumes over which signs (miracles) he did or did not perform. But none dispute the fact that he shared this intimacy with God; it seemed to be the source of all his confidence. Was this faith shaken at the end?

Shaken, yes. Stormed by the powers of hell. Those awful words fell from the cross, "My God, my God, why have you abandoned me?" But his last words in the garden were a surrender to God's will, and on the cross he hands over, in one final act of trust, his dying life to the one he still calls Father.

Perhaps we too have known doubt and denial, and a

scene of torment which yielded finally to surrender and peace. The power is still there to lift us from that black pit of despair which is worse than death itself.

Here is the testimony of another person who underwent a passion. He was a Polish Jew, Yossel Rakover, who died in the Warsaw ghetto in 1943. These words were written on a dirty piece of paper squeezed into a small bottle:

> God, You have done everything to make me stop believing in You. Now, lest it seem to You that You will succeed by these tribulations in driving me from the right path, I notify You, God, and God of my fathers, that it will not avail You in the least. You may insult me. You may castigate me. You may take from me all that I cherish and hold dear in the world. You may torture me to death, but I will always love You and these are my last words to You, my wrathful God:...I die exactly as I have lived, crying, "Eternally praised be the God of the dead, the God of vengeance, of truth, of love, who will soon show His face to the world again and shake its foundations with His almighty voice."

THE RESURRECTION

1 Corinthians 15:35–43

But someone will ask, "How are the dead raised? With what kind of body do they come?" Fool! What you sow does not come to life unless it dies. And as for what you sow, you do not sow the body that is to be, but a bare seed, perhaps of wheat or of some other grain. But God gives it a body as he has chosen, and to each kind of seed its own body. Not all flesh is alike, but there is one flesh for human beings, another for animals, another for birds, and another for fish. There are both heavenly bodies and earthly bodies, but the glory of the heavenly is one thing, and that of the earthly is another. There is one glory of the sun, and another glory of the moon, and another glory of the stars; indeed, star differs from star in glory.

So it is with the resurrection of the dead. What is sown is perishable, what is raised is imperishable. It is sown in dishonor, it is raised in glory. It is sown in weakness, it is raised in power.

THE RESURRECTION
OF THE BODY

What is the human body? Something we feed, rest, use to touch and communicate. Something that weighs us down at times and is subject to disease and pain and mortality. A ballet dancer has one view of her body and a person crippled with arthritis another. The dancer might consider it as a wing to fly, the cripple as a crutch to leave behind. But there is one statement we can make about any body: it is matter. And here the physicist brings us an exciting new knowledge: he tells us that matter is energy. Matter is endlessly in a process of transformation. It is energy taking new forms.

This is somewhat parallel to the statements that the church makes using words like resurrection and assumption. The church is saying that the energy which is "me," and which is not just a soul but a living body, a person, is destined to continue, and even more, to be re-created. To be "trans-formed."

We should not worry as to how our bodies are "reassembled" after death—as if God had to work out some gigantic jigsaw puzzle. The church is not talking of biology but making a doctrinal statement that all human life is capable of being re-created or transformed. In a sublime and personal way it is similar to what is happening all around us right now, as matter changes form. If this happens to rain and snow, to mountains and trees, to caterpillars and acorns, we might be confident that it will happen fittingly to us.

A JOYFUL AWAITING

Listen to these words of a young man dying at the age of forty-seven. Carl Fisher was an auxiliary bishop in Los Angeles, one of eleven black bishops in the United States, and he said, "Although I am still the youngest bishop in California, death is not discouraging for me. My life has been full, and I can hardly wait to be with my God." The archbishop of Los Angeles gave this moving tribute after Fisher died: "As a person and as a bishop, his entire life radiated energy and excitement. Just being with him created a sense of enthusiasm and joy—a contagious spirit of delight in being a disciple of Jesus Christ."

What a way to go. Or better, what a way to live, and to trust in God. Here is another example, from the biography of Johann Sebastian Bach. Did he have a lot to be joyful about? It would seem so: music, marriage, many children, sons who continued his composing genius. And a steady job! Indeed, more than one—he was often on the road as concertmaster or organist. It was after one of those trips—and remember, this was before wireless, telegram, and telephone—that he returned home to discover that his wife and two of his children had died in his absence. What can one say when a night like that descends and leaves one in the darkness? In his diary he wrote these words: "Dear Lord, may my joy not leave me." The words come from the depths of the soul. "May my joy not leave me."

We will be confronted with the travail of life, even as Bach was. It's not a penalty, it just goes with being human!

There may seem to be many reasons why we should not be a joyful people. But we can begin by rejoicing in small things: children's play, the antics of a pet, the wind that invites a sailor, the ocean or stream that calls the fisherman. And bigger things: a perfect day, the experience of love, the birth of a child. And very large things: a savior who promises to share the burden of our lives, and who is the final proof or sign that sin and death need not destroy us. We have reason to be a joyful people. In the end, what a blessing it would be if we could make our own the words of the young bishop: "I can hardly wait to be with my God."

MOURNING

Ecclesiasticus 38:16–20

My son, show tears over a dead man
and intone the lament to show
your own deep grief;
bury his body with due ceremonial,
and do not neglect to honor his grave . . . .
And then be comforted in your sorrow;
for grief can lead to death,
a grief-stricken heart
undermines your strength.
Let grief end with the funeral;
a life of grief oppresses the mind.

BE COMFORTED

We do not hear these words often, although they are from the Bible. The message is, of course, incomplete; it says nothing about the hope of eternal life—partly because the inspired writer lived long before Christ. But we can hear those words and supply our own faith in resurrection, speaking as brothers and sisters of the Risen One whom we call Jesus, our Lord. Surely he is the greatest reason why we should not grieve forever.

"Let grief end with the funeral," the holy writer says. Perhaps that is too soon, but his meaning is that grief should end. And be replaced with what? Not oblivion. We do not mean to blot out the memory of one we have loved, nor to act as if death were not a wound that takes a long time healing. Let grief be replaced finally with what? What else can we possibly feel except sorrow, when we think of our loss? The answer lies in two attitudes or convictions we might strive for. The first is thanksgiving—gratitude for a person's life and what we have shared of it. This is a greater sign of love than grief.

Second, let us try to replace our grief with trust. Call it faith if you wish, because we mean the same: a deep trust, or faith, that the God who gave us life, and life together, will continue these gifts and in his own way overcome death and separation. Perhaps one of our big mistakes in the past was to speculate on how he would do this (and we came up with some dull ideas of heaven—white robes, golden harps, and all the rest). We should concentrate rather on the hope that he will do it—raise us, continue our life in more beautiful ways now hidden from our understanding.

Why should we trust God? The shortest answer is Jesus Christ. We would not even know the name of Jesus if he had died without being raised, if Calvary had not been followed by Easter. He died, but he did not die out; it has been rightly said of him that there is no man who is more alive. No name, at least in the Western world, is more frequently uttered; no greater inspiration, hope, and meaning to life, had ever been infused into whole cultures and passed on to millions of human beings. Jesus lives. Let us trust the Father as he did, and our grief will be less than our faith.

The second reason should appeal to Christian and non-Christian, to all who sense the mystery of life that, for a moment at least, we all possess. Why should we trust the Creator that there will be a continuity to the life we now enjoy, that most certainly seems to end? Because we have made it thus far. We exist. Life is a gift already received. He has called us across a very great chasm, from nothingness to personhood, to exist as humans. Each one of us can say, "Once I was nothing—literally no thing—and now I am." "I am" is one of the names for God, the meaning of Yahweh. Our existence is part of him; as if a human life dips into the vast ocean of the divine. He who has made it possible for each of us to say "I am"—why should now his hand suddenly be shortened or his interest be less? The sun will go out before God ceases to love us.

VARIED THOUGHTS

Journey

All life is a journey. But where do we come from, where are we going? To those who see only the surface of things, the answer is quick: "From the womb to the tomb. We begin in our mother's body and we end in the cemetery." Sometimes they add, "That's it; there's nothing else." The believer has an equally short answer, but it is very different: "We go from God to God." Our journey begins in the mind and heart of God who wills to create us. And our journey ends in the place which Jesus called "my Father's house." He even said, "I go, to prepare a place for you." We give our beloved back to God, trusting in the faithfulness of God.

What Do We Take with Us?

A preacher once said in a funeral sermon, "It is a sobering thought that everything you now own will one day be owned by someone else." A person who heard those words went home, shaken. She looked at her closets. Then at the automobiles in the driveway. Then all around her beautifully furnished house. And her china collection. Even that, even the china, even the Wedgewood, would one day be owned by someone else!

Is there anything we own that no one can take from us, that in some sense goes with us when we die?

Yes. Goodness. The record of our good deeds. Whether or not there is a recording angel, the good one does is forever.

Whatever love has wrought goes with us to the judgment seat, into the presence of the loving and all-holy God.

What of faith? Faith is God's gift to us that we nourish in this life by prayer and worship, by love, and response to his Spirit. Faith cannot be given to another. In this life, faith has been our link to the invisible, the realm we call God, heaven, blessedness, a new creation. The gift of faith is no longer needed when Jesus takes us to the Father. For at that moment faith yields to vision, and death gives way to life.

How Much Have We Loved?

If we knew when we were going to die, we would surely prepare—with a will, an insurance policy, a request for prayers. And perhaps a round of goodbyes, a last good time.

There is one other way to prepare, and we should not neglect it, even if we do not know the day or the hour. The only security, when death does come, is how much we have loved.

Have we fed the hungry, clothed the shivering and the cold? Have we sheltered the homeless, visited the sick and the dying? Have we forgotten that the Savior has said, "When you do it to one of these, the least of my brethren, you do it to me"?

And there are still more questions we could ask ourselves now, or that will be asked of us then. Has love won out over malice and pettiness in our lives? Have we gotten over grudges, forgiven those who have injured us? Are we going into that dark valley with resentment still burning, injustice still rankling in our hearts?

These questions could fill us with remorse. Suppose there is no time to do it over, to live even another day. There is no recourse; the light is failing. Oh yes, there is a way out. Not out of the prison called death that holds us all captive, but a way out of our despair, a way out of our sinfulness. It is very simple—seek forgiveness. And we who perhaps were slow to give it will ourselves receive it; the God of mercy will respond.

Despair and Hope: Purpose to Life

Death is universal. No one has ever been spared, not even God's son. But attitudes toward death are very different. The inscriptions on tombstones often reveal these differences. There is one on a pagan tomb in Rome that says, in Latin, "I was not. I am. I am not. I care not." For all these centuries the words have remained in the stone. One wonders about the author. He must have written his own epitaph. It sounds cynical as well as hopeless; it is a chilling statement.

And for those who believe in God it is not true. A believer could write for his or her last testament, "In the beginning I was part of God. Then God let me join the human family. I was conceived, I was born. I was loved and became a person. Now I leave this family, for a time. I return to God, who is forever."

John Updike wrote this in "On Being a Self Forever," a chapter in his book *Self-Consciousness:*

> It is the self as window on the world that we can't bear to think of shutting . . . the thought of the cosmic party going on without me. The yearning for an afterlife is the opposite of selfish: it is love and praise of the world that we are privileged, in this complex interval of light, to witness and experience.

The Train of Life

This simple story was told by a grandmother to her fourteen-year-old grandson. He couldn't get over his grief at the loss of his best friend in a senseless automobile accident. She said to him:

"Life is like taking a train. Everyone who lives takes it, and the train makes many stops. Some get off early! Some stay on for a very long time! Sooner or later everyone gets off, and whether their journey has been long or short, they have reached their destination. The journey is over; they have arrived. And waiting for them when they get off is God."

In God All Are Alive

St. John Chrysostom, one of the great teachers and fathers of the church, lived over 1500 years ago. These are words from his sermon at his mother's funeral:

"The one whom I knew, and loved, and have lost for awhile, is no longer where she was. She is wherever I am, because she is with God, and God is closer to us than we are to ourselves."

Suffering

We cannot escape suffering in some form and it is no longer viewed as a consequence of original sin. Sometimes it results from sin, but more often, pain is simply part of the way the world is made. Suffering then becomes a test of faith. It also brings about a great compassion, untold acts of goodness by those who, like Simon, help us to bear the cross. It is fitting that the dying are blessed with the cross, and often take comfort from the crucifix. It is fitting that the image of the Crucified One often rests on their casket, or is placed in their hands, and the cross goes before them in the rite of Christian burial. It is fitting because Jesus' death is not the end, nor is our death the last word. God has the last word.

The Divine Love Seeks Us

There is a saying which goes like this: A lost thing I could never find, nor a broken thing mend. It seems true for many of us—there are things we lose and do not find, even with the help of St. Anthony! And in the end we lose those we love. Sometimes a friendship is broken, never to be mended. And finally, for each of us the thread of life is broken.

But none of this is true of God, and the children of God. The Divine Love seeks us, even as the woman sought the precious coin, and the father sought his far-away son. And the Divine Mercy which forgives all sins mends all that is broken, and makes it whole at last.

Expectation

A penetrating discussion of resurrection has been given by H.A. Williams in his book, *True Resurrection*. He writes: "The miracle of our being given life beyond the grave is not greater than the miracle of our continually being given life here. Creativity is ever one and the same. It is always the calling into being of the non-existent; and to those who are created it means forever receiving what forever is being given. If in this life we know that we are poor, that we are nothing and have nothing which we are not receiving from the unknown, then it will not seem uniquely strange that life should continue to be given beyond the boundaries of physical death."

ONE WITH GOD

We hope for such impossible things (like immortality) and receive such awesome titles like "the children of God." There is no way these can have validity unless we are part of the One who can do all things, who is all things. Remember the story of the flea who rode on the elephant's back? When they crossed a bridge the flea liked to say, "We sure made those timbers rattle, didn't we?" Our situation is not so different! Or take, for example, an ocean wave. Without the ocean there is no wave. It is part of the sea and belongs to it. The wave rises out of the ocean, subsists in it, and returns to the immensity and calm of the deep. A wave has no enduring power by itself. But it has awesome power as part of the mighty sea.

We are not powerful by ourselves. Indeed we are as insignificant as fleas or drops of water. But it is not the elephant or the ocean that gives strength or greatness. It is the immense universe of divine love, revealed in Jesus, a love which includes us. It is a love which bears us aloft, as the eagle carries her young; a love which becomes a voice calling us sons and daughters, beloved, dear to the heart of the Most High.

PART OF GOD

The portrait of who we are is both terrifying and sublime. We are powerful, and yet we die. We love, and we also hate. We look up to the stars, but we cannot even count them, and before long the stars look down on our dust. We live, but apparently we live for no more than a visible moment in ten billion years of time. The words of an ancient favorite hymn tried to express something more:

> Ages are coming, roll on and vanish:
> children will follow where fathers passed;
> never our pilgrim song, joyful and
> heaven-borne,
> will cease while time and mountains last.

But when they do not? When time is no more, and mountains slide into the sea, or vanish themselves—what then of the human?

The shortest answer is that each person is part of God, and God is everlasting.

LIFE IS ETERNAL

(The following appeared some years ago on a card published by Marjorie Heath; text attributed to "author unknown." In one way or another the metaphor here has often been used to express hope in the continuity of life, the sense of "other worlds," and the smallness of our vision.)

I am standing upon the seashore. A ship at my side spreads her white sails to the morning breeze and starts for the blue ocean. She is an object of beauty and strength and I stand and watch her until at length she hangs like a speck of white cloud just where the sea and sky come down to mingle with each other. Then someone at my side says, "There! She's gone."

Gone where? Gone from my side, that is all. She is just as large in mast and hull and spar as she was when she left my side, and just as able to bear her load of living freight to the place of destination. Her diminished size is in me, not in her; and just at the moment when someone at my side says, "There! She's gone," there are other eyes watching her coming, and other voices ready to take up the glad shout, "There she comes!"

The ship that passes over the horizon
is lost to our sight.
But it goes on;
it continues to its destination
and a safe harbor at last.
Beyond that horizon are other worlds
that welcome the traveler.
We live with the conviction
or struggle with the hope
that life itself is an horizon,
and our journey goes beyond it
not to darkness but to life.

CREATIVE POWER

Consider the birth of a child—is this an adequate sign of the resurrection and of hope? It is only if we understand that any newly born child manifests the power of the Creator at work. It is a power that brings forth life, that makes things new. And this eventually includes the body, the form of expression for a human being which has to be made new at a person's death. Why should it happen? The question is really, why should it not happen? This creative power of which we speak, through the human agency of parenthood, has brought each one of us from non-being to being. The bridge of existence has been crossed. And this is a much greater transition than to pass from one shape of existence to another—a statement we make in our funeral liturgy, that "To your faithful, Lord, life is changed, not taken away." We have a good existential reason for believing this. Once we were not; now we are. If God was with us in the beginning, there is no reason, from what we have seen of God in Jesus and his love for us, to think God will be absent or powerless at this new stage in our growth.

DEATH IS HOMECOMING

Abraham Heschel was more than a great Jewish scholar; he was a mystic whose faith in God was so deep he could write these words: "When life is an answer, death is a homecoming."

But to what is life an answer? Not to a question, at least not to many questions which remain unanswered, such as the suffering of the innocent, or why we are made in this in-between fashion. Those questions lie buried in the soul, to be answered only in another phase of our existence. Life is not an answer to a question but to an invitation. It is an invitation to accept the gift and the One who gives it.

Another mystic expressed that answer in beautiful words which are often quoted. It is Dag Hammarskjöld who wrote, "For all that has been, thanks; for all that will be, yes."

Heschel could speak this way even though his family, clan, and the culture of his youth were destroyed in the satanic flames of the Holocaust. And Hammarskjöld could speak thus in spite of great loneliness in his life and many frustrations, a life that ended in a plane crash while on a U.N. mission at the height of his unfinished career. Each of these men believed that God is loving and giving, not just being, and this belief can be so strong that it overcomes the doubt and the darkness.

A Hasidic teacher says that mourning takes place on three levels: silence, tears, and song. Silence we know, for there are no words that can express our love for those who grieve. The words that finally help are the words of God that come to us from revelation and ritual. They express the promise that God alone can fulfill, and they offer the peace that God alone can give. Silence. Silence before the mystery of life, and the One who holds all things, life, death, and the future in his hands.

As for tears, they are not a sign of weakness but of love. The wise man wrote in Ecclesiasticus (38:16–20): "My son, show tears over a dead man and intone the lament to show your own deep grief; bury his body with due ceremonial, and do not neglect to honor his grave . . ."

Can anything more be said? Yes—some writers now speak of the "tears of God" who shares our pain.

As for song, does our mourning dare move to this level? Is there not something in music or song that expresses our grief but infuses it with hope? Think of the songs we have heard or sung which are associated with death or funerals. Sometimes it will be a great soprano singing the faith of Job in the passage from Handel's *Messiah*: "I know that my Redeemer liveth." Or two songs used so often now at funerals, "Be Not Afraid" and "I Am the Bread of Life." Or the Good Shepherd psalm. Or the traditional Gregorian chant, "In Paradisum": "Go forth to paradise, and may the angels take you by the hand." Or the hymn of Easter, "Jesus Christ Is Risen Today." These are songs more of life than of death. There is no night that does not yield finally to the dawn. And death is overcome by the One who calls us to live not in darkness but in the day. We mourn in silence. And with tears. And with song.

A BAFFLING DEATH

The following letter was written and quickly faxed to the five children of a man who inexplicably took his own life. His wife—their mother—had died of cancer the year before, but he had given no sign of despondency that would lead to suicide. The priest in dispatching the letter (and, later, conducting the funeral), was well aware that it would be shared with relatives who would be troubled by the older teaching of the churches on suicide. These are words of comfort, yes, but also, they reflect the current thinking of the Christian churches on this tragic form of death.

My heart is with you, but so is my head, my thinking, and I want to share these thoughts with all of you. I am speaking as a theologian and teacher in the Church, as well as your friend. First, do not doubt in the least the fact of your father's salvation. He is with God; he is more alive than we are; he is home, and well.

It doesn't matter what older Catholics may have heard about tragic death and the way these things were handled in the past. We have a new understanding of salvation and God's mercy—and also of how our freedom in making choices is limited by the pressures of life.

I repeat: you don't have to die with the sacraments, you don't have to die with prayer on your lips, to be acceptable to God. These things are wonderful when they are present. But if they are not present, the love of God is still unlimited, and God understands human frailty more than we do.

Try not to dwell too much on what happened, or seek to explain it. Many things in life remain a mystery. There is a mystery of evil and suffering that touches us all. The only thing that keeps us sane, and willing to go on, is that the mystery of love is greater. And God is at the heart of this love. The God of life, in whom your parents now abide.

It is helpful to think only of good things, to try to block out dark and brooding thoughts. You have the gift of life from your parents, the knowledge that you were cherished and esteemed. You have each other, and your future, for which they prepared you so well. And you have us, who are privileged to be your friends. When you are tempted to think of sad things or to ask the painful questions—why do these things happen?—it may be helpful to repeat a favorite prayer or poem, to think of a beautiful experience, or just to repeat a single word, perhaps God, or Jesus, or Mary. Anything that cleanses the mind, and opens yourself to the gift of peace, or God's presence.

We try too much to understand things, and forget that God stands under our whole existence. There is no place to fall except into God's hands.

I know that words, including these, and even the word of God you will hear in church, do not mean much when grief is strong. But eventually the meaning lays hold of us, and brings comfort. I pray that it will be that way with you. So I want to tell you again, and I feel that the Holy Spirit is helping me to tell you this: your parents are alive, not dead; they are with God, and one day we will share that life, and understand.

Your parents were good and loving people, and in the end, that is all that counts. So as soon as you can, return to happy and useful lives. This is what they would wish. This is our wish, and God's will for you.

Father Nolan

THE YEARNING OF THE SUN

This verse from D. H. Lawrence calls for much thought:

> Thou shalt fight
> as a flower fighteth upwards
> through the stones . . .
> to flower in the sun at last—
> for the yearning of the Lord
> streameth as a sun
> even upon the stones.

Of whom is he talking? Think of the first struggle we make just to live, to be born. We succeed, but human life is fragile; it has its brief moment in the sun, and then, darkness. Or that would be our story except for Jesus Christ. Think of his Easter victory when the Father raised him up to a new creation beyond sin and death. Jesus is Lord. They had sealed his grave with a stone but "the yearning of God" is to show us definitively, in the act of resurrection, that the divine power which is love is powerful even over "the last of the enemies" which is death.

And that victory is also ours; Christ is the firstborn of the dead. Life is the Creator's first gift to us, we value it dearly, and no stone weighs more heavily upon us than the death of the beloved. But "the yearning of the Lord streameth as a sun even upon the stones." It is the Divine Love that draws us forth to be children of the light.

IMAGES OF ETERNITY

I could tell you of a good man
who befriended many, and was beloved by many,
and who suffered much before he came to die.
His name? His name is Jesus. Jesus Christ.

Today, his name could also be _____
a good man who befriended many.
How many? They know,
    and God knows.
It is good deeds like his that open the gates.
He was beloved by many. Especially...
And yet with all this,
he suffered much before he came to die.

His story is like Jesus.
Of course, because he belonged to him.
He joined his church through Baptism.
He sought to follow his teaching, the gospel, in his life.

In each case—Jesus, our friend today, your parents,
    yourself someday—
you have a right to ask: why? Why do the good suffer?
Why does anyone die?

The answer is a mystery.
It is part of the mystery of pain and evil.

It is a mystery we cannot solve.
It forces us to trust, to make an act of faith,
that God is still good, and has other plans for us.
The reason we can live with hope
is that we have also experienced the mystery of love—
of God's love, revealed to us in Jesus Christ,
God's love, of which you yourselves are the sign,
in your affection and concern,
in your deep love for each other.
Indeed, that is the last, best service
you give to those you have loved,
if you survive them.
At their bedside, in their pain, in all your vigils,
you have been a sign of God's love,
the love that is greater than all.
St. Paul once wrote, in words that sound like trumpets,

> For I am convinced
> that neither death, nor life,
> nor angels, nor rulers,
> nor things present, nor things to come,
> nor powers, nor height, nor depth,
> nor anything else in all creation,
> will be able to separate us
> from the love of God
> in Christ Jesus our Lord.
>   *Romans 8:38–39*

It is this love that wins the victory,
and enables us to live with hope.

There are two brief metaphors

that may help us to understand these thoughts,
to see more clearly the nature of our journey,
the adventure, the human pilgrimage to God.

One is the river.
It rises in far-off places, from tiny springs and brooklets.
It gathers strength and power,
moves swiftly along its appointed course.
At times there is a stormy passage:
winds, waves, rough waters.
But in the end?
In the end, all rivers flow into the sea.
There is a moment when the waters join,
when you can still see both river and ocean.
But then they are merged; there is only one.
We need an angel to tell us,

So is your life, O child of God!
It rises in far-off places
in a moment of desire.
It is fed and nourished
by the deep springs of affection, of friendship and love.
A human life gathers strength and power,
runs its appointed course.
It goes through difficult passages, storms and rough waters.
But in the end?
As the river comes to the sea, so the pilgrim comes to God.
We are joined to the greatness,
the wideness of God's mercy,
and the fullness of God's life.

Some day come down to the sea;
you will see a ship set sail for the horizon.
Soon it passes over and is lost to our sight.
But it continues on to its destination
and a safe harbor at last.
Beyond that horizon are other worlds
that welcome the traveler.

And we who are left behind, who remain on the shore?
We live with the conviction, or struggle with the hope
that life itself is an horizon,
and our journey goes beyond it
not to darkness but to life.

RESURRECTION

This moving letter (in *Commonweal*, Sept. 6, 1985, by Lawrence D. Hogan, Jr.) followed a heavy discussion of what happens when we die:

> I have a card in my wallet that I pull out from time to time. It reads, "In Memory Of Lawrence D. Hogan, Sr., born August 23, 1901, died June 29, 1978"; and below that the inscription is, "If we die with Christ, we shall live with him, and if we are faithful to the end, we shall reign with him."
> I turn it over and find much delight in words attributed to Thomas More, "Pray for me as I will for thee, that we may merrily meet in heaven."

Mr. Hogan then quoted the following from W.E.B. DuBois' eulogy for Alexander Crummell. It describes DuBois' last moments with his friend, and his hopes for the meeting with Christ in eternal life:

> He sat one morning gazing toward the sea. He smiled and said, "The gate is rusty on the hinges." That night at star-rise a wind came moaning out of the west to blow the gate ajar, and then the soul I loved fled like a flame across the Seas, and in its seat sat Death.
> I wonder where he is today? I wonder if in that

dim world beyond, as he came gliding in, there rose on some wan throne a King—a dark and pierced Jew, who knows the writings of the earthly damned, saying, as he laid those heart-wrung talents down, "Well done!" while round about the morning stars sat singing.

TIME AND ETERNITY

We are creatures of time, and it is forever passing. It is not a river in which we can stand still; we move in this current to the end of time. And what is that? Eternity. Eternal life is not duration; it is completion: a present in which all that is good and of God is present to us. We experience it momentarily or at least by analogy in this life. We can best understand with the help of the poets; consider these five lines from Henry Van Dyke which were read at the funeral of Princess Diana:

> Time is too slow for those who wait,
> too swift for those who fear,
> too long for those who grieve,
> too short for those who rejoice,
> but for those who love, time is eternity.

(In Van Dyke's version it simply says "time is not.")

This sense of escaping time, or the body, and tasting eternity now, is reflected in *Four Quartets*, by T.S. Eliot: "...music heard so deeply / That it is not heard at all, but you are the music / While the music lasts." And in this poem by Theodore Spencer:

> The day was a year at first
> when children ran in the garden;
> the day shrank down to a month
> when the boys played ball.
>
> The day was a week thereafter
> when young men walked in the garden;
> the day was itself a day
> when love grew tall.
>
> The day shrank down to an hour
> when old men limped in the garden;
> the day will last forever
> when it is nothing at all.

THE COMING OF
THE SON OF MAN

But in those days, after that suffering, the sun will be darkened, and the moon will not give its light, and the stars will be falling from heaven, and the powers in the heavens will be shaken. Then they will see "the Son of Man coming in clouds" with great power and glory. Then he will send out the angels, and gather his elect from the four winds, from the ends of the earth to the ends of heaven. From the fig tree learn its lesson: as soon as its branch becomes tender and puts forth its leaves, you know that summer is near. So also, when you see these things taking place, you know that he is near, at the very gates. Truly I tell you, this generation will not pass away until all these things have taken place. Heaven and earth will pass away, but my words will not pass away.

But about that day or hour no one knows, neither the angels in heaven, nor the Son, but only the Father.

Mark 13:24–32

WHAT PASSES AWAY?

In approaching the Scriptures it is often necessary to put the text in context. We need especially to do that with the style of writing called apocalyptic.

There are two reference points for this passage: one is an event which has already happened—the destruction of the Temple in 70 A.D., a time of great upheaval and disaster. The other event was expected but did not happen; it is called the *parousia*, or the Second Coming, a time of fulfillment which the early Christians thought was just around the corner. We do not place great emphasis today on the Second Coming. It's there, in our Creed: "He will come again, to judge the living and the dead." But when, we do not know—he even tells us that.

Most people, including believers, fear death. That may be part of the mechanism of survival; fearing death in the five o'clock rush hour can help to make us good drivers! There is an oft-quoted statement by psychiatrist Carl Jung that no one over forty ever came to him with a problem that was not rooted somehow in the awareness that death was approaching. There is an inescapability about our fate that was never put better than by an unknown scribe in India five centuries before Christ. He wrote, "Not in the sky, not in the midst of the sea, not even in the clefts of the mountains is there a spot in the whole world where, if a man abide there, death could not overtake him."

"If a man abide there," he says. The whole lesson of our rather swift passage is that we do not abide; we pass. The whole meaning of faith is that we pass over, but can we hold this with serenity? When that hidden time occurs, do we go to destiny, or doom, to reunion or to separation, to dissolution, or a new creation? All Christian faith cries out that we live, we live in Christ who alone abides. It is his word that does not pass away, and we believe his word has taken flesh and lives in us—even in our mortality.

We do not doubt what our faith teaches and what we celebrate each Easter and with each Eucharist. But we need to face what might be called our existential fear. We are made to live, we are sustained by the earth and its people, and the thought of loss, even transition, is shuddering. Perhaps God made us this way to test us. Our passage is usually not like the light gently fading. It is a wrenching, a tearing out of roots. And it is a final act of faith.

Jesus says that no matter what the terrors of the night—or day—his word will not pass away. It is his word that assures us of rescue, and resurrection. And it is possible to believe this so strongly that fear, even fear of dying, is finally banished. Here is the testimony of a great Christian shortly before his death. Fr. Karl Rahner, S.J., one of the world's eminent scholars, wrote deep theology. But of dying he could write like this:

> Let us therefore run forward, singing: It is good! And for him who runs to meet God nothing is past and lost forever. God has already bestirred himself and is quite near in the impatience of that love that makes all things new. He is near! Our past fickleness is the starting point of the eternal God. Glad tiding! We are running towards God—and he is already near.

A POET AND A
THEOLOGIAN ON EASTER

Even those who have not read Dante's *Divine Comedy* may know that it includes an imaginative tour of hell, purgatory, and heaven. Dante is a very great artist; his sublime epic poem is certainly inspired, and its author hoped it was a form of revelation, a metaphoric way of hinting at the truth which is of God. We are caught up with Dante's great vision; this is how he moves—or is moved—to describe the first sound of paradise that he hears. It is not the singing of hymns; it is not music at all. "It seemed to me," he wrote, "like the laughter of the universe."

We are not at ease with laughter in reference to sacred things; it does not seem reverent. We do not even understand how or why the Greeks, and Dante, use the word comedy (they thought of all events as either tragic or comic). For us a comedian is someone who tells jokes. In the Christ-story, the joke is on those who thought their power could destroy him. Christ and his disciples have the last laugh, even though they die the death. But it is not the kind of laughter that taunts one's enemies. It is like the laughter at a birthday party where we celebrate the gift of life.

Theologian Harvey Cox reflects on Dante's "laughter of the universe" in the light of Easter (he does this in a superb Easter sermon written for *Christianity in Crisis*, 4/6/87). His insights help us to understand Easter and also to enjoy it.

First, he says that the sin and evil still so prevalent in our world are certainly nothing to laugh about. It might, to use human language, seem mean of God to sit up there in heaven and laugh. The psalmist uses just those words (Psalm 2:4): "The Holy One who sitteth in the heavens shall laugh." But Cox sees two reasons why it is all right. "The laughter of God, as the passion accounts tell us, does not come from afar. It does not emanate from One who can safely chortle, from a safe distance, at another's pain. It comes from One who has also felt the hunger pangs, the hurt of betrayal by friends and the torturer's torch." And, "God laughs, it seems, because he knows how it will all turn out in the end."

And we are reminded of the *Magnificat*, the song of Mary: "He has brought down the powerful from their thrones, and lifted up the lowly." Or the words of faith uttered by God's servant Job: "I know that my Redeemer liveth, and I shall be clothed with my flesh on the last day" (Job 19:25).

When we go through Holy Week, Cox says, "We recount the tale of a man who sided with the disinherited and the heartbroken, who became the hope of those who had lost all hope, who was tortured to death and sealed in a tomb." We read the gospel accounts of the Passion and we move through a pattern of prayer called the Stations or the Way of the Cross. There was another kind of laughter during the Passion of Jesus, but it was raucous, mean-spirited, brutal. It came from the soldiers when they dressed him up as king with a reed for a sceptre and a circlet of thorns for a crown. It also came from the onlookers as they jeered him, helpless on the cross. Then it all ended. Or, as Cox writes, "The raucous howls of the executioners stopped only when they finally grew weary. The obscene hoots of the passersby ended at last when the figure on the cross would not rail back. The sneers of Pilate and the jeers of Herod also subsided when, their official duties finished, they returned to their palaces having rid themselves once and for all—so they thought—of this troublemaker."

Where is the laughter? It comes with the surprise ending. It comes with the joy of Easter morn. It is the symbol of God's victory. It is the laughter of those who are happy, beyond pain, sin, death, and even time. It is the sound of those who dance, sing, play, and enjoy each other. Our existence now is like a wound-up clock; it is running down. And our laughter is often interrupted. But some day, beyond the clock of time, it will be joined to the glad sound that Dante heard as he drew near paradise.

FAITH, HOPE, AND LOVE

The belief in personal resurrection, life beyond death, grew slowly in Israel. It is given vivid expression in the second book of the Maccabees, in the Hebrew Scriptures, which describes the martyrdom of seven brothers. One of them said to his tormentors, "You are depriving us of this present life, but the King of the world will raise us up to live again forever." And another: "It is my choice to die at the hands of men with the God-given hope of being restored to life by him." The mother, who was also put to death, exhorted her sons; she referred to the miracle of their birth and said, "The Creator of the world, who has shaped the beginning of humankind and devised the origin of all things, will in his mercy give life and breath back to you again."

This was all before Jesus, long before his death and resurrection. Where did the Maccabees get this faith in life beyond death? The young brother called it "a God-given hope."

Their words move us—or perhaps they shame us. We are the heirs of a resurrection faith. We celebrate Easter and Christ's victory all our lives. Yet many of us do not live with that calm confidence or expectation that a new dimension or experience of life awaits us when we die. Why is this? Take a walk through a cemetery and read the inscriptions. Some express the faith and hope we are talking about, but not many, especially today. Others even mock the bystander, the sort of inscription that says,

"Where I am, you too shall be." Not a very cheerful thought. Many just record the fact of birth and death of someone who presumably now is "gone with the wind." But that is not, cannot, be true for the believer. "The just are in the hands of God, and no torment shall touch them." That, too, is in the Old Testament, not the New. We sit in church at funerals and hear these words and many others, equally full of promises. But even though it is God who is promising, we are still of many minds about the thought of death. Why?

Love is one reason. We are quite literally loved into being, into personhood. And the relationships that form in life—between husband and wife or parent and child, for instance—are so strong that we cannot bear the thought that they will end, at least in this present world that we know. And even if we accept death for ourselves, we cannot readily accept it for those we love. Even the prospect of our own dying may sadden us for a very human reason; it brings grief to those dear to us. William Shakespeare, the greatest poet of the English language, put that thought in sublime words:

> No longer grieve for me when I am dead.
> Nay, if you read these lines, remember not
> the hand that wrote them. I love you so
> that I, in your sweet thoughts would be forgot
> if thinking on me then should make you woe.

"I love you so." There is the cause of our pain—but also of our hope. God can say, "I love you so that I would have you with me." There is a magnificent passage in the book of Wisdom (Wisdom 11:22—12:1) which speaks of God as infinite, the creator, all-powerful. But in the midst of that praise, which is also echoed in the psalms, there is the simple declaration that "You love all things that are, and loathe nothing you have made." We should think about that, and take heart. We love our own creations—a poem we have made, or a table, or a loaf of bread, and above all a child, made in our own image. Isn't it the same with God, only more so? Parent as well as power, God is lover as well as creator. Moses called him the God of people, people with names.

Go back again to those confident words from 2 Maccabees: "the God-given hope of being restored to life." We cannot really prove immortality, at least make an airtight case for it. It remains a mystery, and faith in the resurrection, even faith in God, continues to be a gift, for which we can at least prepare by opening our hearts. But what we cannot prove we can often feel in the depths of our being. Shakespeare also wrote of death in *King Lear*. When the king mourns his daughter with a terrible grief, he asks if it is right that a tree, a bird, an insect should live, and his beloved Cordelia should be dead. A realist would say, "All things die."

But, as a great Christian thinker has said, they die "into God." That way of expressing it, or the phrase "eternal life," is the best that can be done with words. We do not die into nothingness but into God. If all things come from God, isn't it reasonable to assume that all things return to God? There is a hint of that thinking—and believing—in the words of the young brother as he held out his hands to the tormentors and said, "It was from Heaven that I received these." Each one of us can say that it is from God we have received existence, being, the capacity to speak and laugh. It is from God that we inherit the earth and all of our faculties, no matter how much we misuse these gifts. And God, as Jesus declared, "is not the God of the dead but of the living" (Luke 20:38). For him—and in him—all are alive.

THE ETERNITY OF LOVE

Ursula Niebuhr, a well-educated, sensitive woman, considered herself a Christian, a believer, but had difficulty accepting the resurrection. She said that Easter in the churches appeared to be little more than a style show, and the sermons did not help; many of them seemed to be celebrating or talking about a rite of spring.

She discussed her doubts with her husband (who was Reinhold Niebuhr, one of this century's great Christian thinkers). He said that perhaps she should not try to find answers by asking questions but seek the answers through the liturgy, the worship, especially the music. Then he added that music helps the most, especially if you don't understand the words.

So they went to a "liturgical church" for Easter. Still she was not satisfied. But she said, as the years went on, "Some of my Easters have been full of dyings and death." Some of her friends died, and then her husband passed on. It came to her that she could believe far more easily in the eternity of love than the immortality of the soul. She added that whatever is good, and true, and beautiful abides, and there is a feeling—she called it an instinct—that those who express the good, as Jesus did, also abide. She called them "pointers to the realm of the mysterious transcendent."

Yes, it is the way deep thinkers talk about God, or the Risen Christ.

MY GRACE IS SUFFICIENT

All life is precious, any untimely death is tragic. One thinks immediately of Job when one hears of this man who lost, in one swift, terrible automobile accident, his wife, mother, and daughter. His name is Jerry Sittser, and he finally wrote his thoughts in a book, *A Grace Disguised*. It is an invaluable testament—ultimately to grace. But let him tell it.

First he relates the many comments and letters he received which said what happened to him was so unfair. One of them wrote, "Your family appeared so ideal. This tragedy is a terrible injustice. If it can happen to you, it can happen to any of us. Now no one is safe!"

He pondered that, undoubtedly through many tears, and finally thought, "No one is safe, because the universe is hardly a safe place. It is often mean, unpredictable, and unjust. Loss has little to do with our notions of fairness. Some people live long and happily, though they deserve to suffer. Others endure one loss after another, though they deserve to be blessed. Loss is no more a respecter of persons and positions than good fortune is. There is often no rhyme or reason to the misery of some and to the happiness of others."

So does he agree with this judgment that life is unfair, God is unjust? Not that God is unjust, no, but his answer does not express a blind faith. He writes, "Over time I began to be bothered by the assumption that I had a right to complete fairness. Granted, I did not deserve to lose three members of my family. But then again, I am not sure I deserved to have them in the first place."

He thinks back on the three he had lost: an endearing wife, a mother who had "lived well and served people through her life's end," and sustained him during a rebellious youth, and a daughter who, as children do, filled their life with excitement. Then he concludes, "Perhaps I did not deserve their deaths; but I did not deserve their presence in my life, either. On the face of it, living in a perfectly fair world appeals to me. But deeper reflection makes me wonder. In such a world I might never experience tragedy; but neither would I experience grace, especially the grace God gave me in the form of the three wonderful people whom I lost."

Is there anything more to say? Yes, a conclusion that invites us to think deeply and pray about what we have read, because it is the ultimate answer, the same answer St. Paul gave when, speaking for God, the apostle said, "My grace is sufficient for thee." This wounded believer, who thinks so well, concludes: "So, God spare us a lifetime of fairness! To live in a world with grace is better by far than to live in a world of absolute fairness. A fair world might make life nice for us, but only as nice as we are. We might get what we deserve, but I wonder how much that is and whether or not we would really be satisfied. A world with grace will give us more than we deserve. It will give us life, even in our suffering."

MORE FROM KARL RAHNER

The Jesuit priest thought and wrote so deeply that a standard joke was that his brother translated his heavy thinking from German into German! But this translation comes through to us with clear, ringing jubilation. He was coming to the end of his life, and tries to explain, as much as any of us can, what happens when we die:

> And then in a shattering shout of joy it turns out that the vast silent emptiness which we experience as death is filled with the Mystery of mysteries whom we call God . . . filled with his pure light and all embracing love.
>
> Eighty years is a long time. However for each one, the life span allotted to him or her is but a brief moment during which what should be at last *becomes.*

Dare we comment? Becomes what?

A life beyond pain, beyond the need of healing,
    because nothing is broken.
A time when love is not afraid,
    and happiness unshadowed.
A time when there is no time,
      when the "Being that let us be"
now completes our existence.

AN EASTER FAITH

It is in the verses of Shakespeare,
our greatest poet,
that we find the vainest wish:
speaking, as poets do, to his beloved, he says,

> Shall I compare thee to a summer's day?
> Thou art more lovely, and more temperate.

And then he reaches for the sky, the moon, for the illusion.

He sings,

> Thy eternal summer shall not fade
> Nor shall death brag thou wanderest in her shade.

It is not true—how sadly we come to know that. The seasons of the year serve to remind us of our own life cycle: spring, its glory all around us, is the time of birth and youth; summer, the fullness of one's life, the ripening of powers; autumn is aging, wisdom, harvest; and winter brings the chill of death.

"Thy eternal summer shall not fade." But it does.
We see it every year, in ourselves, and those around us.
All that are born grow older.
All live under the same sentence of death.

And yet all have inherited
the same promise of life from Jesus.
"I came that you may have life,
and have it more abundantly."

Our living and our longing
are at odds with our mortality.
Nothing, not even the universe,
billions of years old, can be forever.
Unless, unless—
everything is part of Being,
part of the One who is.

Our lives have been compared to waves
that hasten to the pebbled shore,
disperse, and are no more.

Faith gives another message.
It speaks of Jesus' victory, which is also ours.
It promises another life.
Or rather, the completion and perfection
of the one we are living now.
Can it be that this clutch of years, these rushing days,
this piece of time that is our portion,
is only the beginning,
that life is ahead of us, not behind us?

This Easter, and every Eucharist, is a feast of love.
Love is our shorthand for what we mean by God.
The apostle Paul once wrote,
in a burst of words like the sound of trumpets,
"Nothing in life or death shall be able to separate us
from the love which God has revealed to us
in Christ Jesus our Lord!"

Jesus is God's love embodied.
Love that became vulnerable, even unto death.
Love that emptied itself that all might be filled.
The saints say of God that in his will we find our peace.
It is in his love that we find our hope.
For that love is also power, God's power;
it created the world,
and in raising Jesus from the dead, and promising our own,
it moves to a new dimension.

It is that love which sends the Spirit into our lives,
the Spirit that assures us we are forgiven,
that we too are raised up, we too are empowered.
We are **in Christ**,
and nothing shall separate us, in life or death.

The poet we have quoted is the author of the famous lines,

> For thy sweet love remembered
> such wealth brings
> That then I scorn to change
> my state with kings.

We can say this most of Jesus
who has invaded our hearts.
Love willing to die for us,
willing to forgive us,
waiting to embrace us
in the life we call eternal
when we are home with God.

JTN

QUESTIONS—
ON LOVE AND TRUST

Here is a statement that could be biblical, that could have come from one of the prophets. It is food for the journey, bread of life:

> I am obliged to believe in an abyss of love which is deeper than the abyss of death: I dare not lose faith in that love. I sink into death, eternal death, if I do. I must feel that this love is compassing the universe. More about it I cannot know. God knows. I leave myself all to him.
>
> *F.D. Maurice*

Not everyone agrees. We are surrounded by many people who accept, with resignation or despair, that death is final. When the writer Stewart Alsop knew he was terminally ill, he was interviewed by Dick Cavett. Both of them agreed that they did not believe in life after death, not because they did not wish to, but because they found it too difficult to accept.

What does this passage suggest to us? That Jesus has given the definitive witness of this all-encompassing love? Is this what experience suggests—have we been touched by love and what love has wrought, held by it so powerfully that we really doubt in our hearts that death can destroy it? And not love in the abstract but loving persons. Is this why the philosopher Maurice Blondel wrote in a play, "To love someone is to say that thou—at least thou—shall not die"? Isn't this the challenge of the whole biblical statement, the entire revelation of Israel and Jesus the Christ? Jesus exemplifies the great breakthrough verses that conclude the Song of Songs (8:6–7): "For Love is strong as Death.... The flash of it is a flame of fire, a flame of Yahweh himself. Love no flood can quench, no torrents drown."

Have we not good reason to "leave myself all to him?" We make acts of trust every day that hold our lives in the balance. When we enter an airplane we leave all to the pilot because we are powerless and he is knowledgeable. Must we not do the same in the journey called life, even for a single day, even to close our eyes in a night's sleep? What does it mean to address the Master of the Universe, eternal God, by a gentle word like "Father"? Jesus taught us the word, and we trust him. We experience all life as a gift; we see the earth itself turn from the burial place of seed to become a garden of life. We know that power encompasses the universe; it balances the planets and moves the sun. Is it not possible that the ultimate form of this power is love, a love so powerful that it swallows up sin and death? When we die, do we surrender to death, or to God?

AWAKENING FROM DEATH

The apostle Paul wrote, "I would not have you ignorant concerning those who sleep in death." When he goes on to talk about heaven he uses standard biblical images which are not very appealing—a trumpet sounding, clouds underfoot, ascending into the air. But he is more on target in calling death a sleep. Jesus used the same expression when they told him his friend Lazarus had died, and also when he restored to life the daughter of the synagogue ruler.

To equate death with sleep in this context is not a mere figure of speech. For those who believe, it says something about God's power. There is certainly no human power which can wake the dead. But "with God there is no death"—or, as other translations put it, "for God all are alive" (Luke 20:38). Those words are a calm, triumphal assertion that death has no finality or power over the Lord of life.

Recently, Karl Rahner, the German Jesuit theologian, left us on the swift journey to God. Rahner was a towering intellect, a giant of thinking and believing. His going left a great gap—like a tree, a redwood or sequoia, that is felled and leaves a torn and wounded space in the landscape. Rahner was the author of a whole library of books and articles. His writing was usually heavy, for scholars to ponder. But this is the gist of what he said, three months before his dying, for believers—and mortals—to ponder.

He first of all declared that the concept of eternal life has

70

been trivialized. One could say that this is true even of St. Paul's attempt to talk about it as a meeting with the Lord "in the air." But this trivialization has happened, Rahner continues, because "it is an unspeakable wonder that the absolute Godhead has descended, simply and directly, into the narrow realm of our creaturehood." He confesses that he and all other contemporary theologians have failed to find the right words, the right model, to represent eternal life to believers today.

But then he tries. He speaks of God as a vast and silent emptiness, and a human life as one brief moment or irruption of freedom. It is indeed brief, only a moment of time, but during that moment "question turned into answer, possibility into actuality, time into eternity, freedom offered into freedom obtained." (When does this happen? Is it not in the moment of dying, when time itself dies and life is no longer bounded?) Does the great thinker, this mortal theologian who perhaps surmised that he was about to test his own theories, say anything more? Yes. Rahner spoke of "a vast empty silence." That description would be frightening if he did not add his further conviction that it is precisely "this emptiness which we experience as death which is filled with the mystery of mysteries which we call God, filled with his pure light and his all-embracing and bestowing love." Another theologian, Hans Küng, calls this "dying into God."

Rahner puts the word "God" in quotes, because all words fail when we try to express the Infinite, when time and time's creatures reach for eternity. But we do try, for as Paul declared, "We would have you be clear about those who sleep in death, otherwise you might yield to grief like those who have no hope."

71

A CHILDREN'S SERMON

The Hottentot people in Africa have a traditional story about the moon. It seems that the moon wished to send a message to humankind. The message was very important; it went like this: "Just as every night I die, and dying, rise, so you, too, will die, and dying, rise." (The message seems clear. Every night, if we stay up long enough, we can see the moon grow pale and finally disappear. But then it's back again the next night. It's just been gone from sight for a while.) The moon chose the ant to deliver the message, and the ant was very slow. The rabbit ran by and said, "Here, I'll deliver the message." He did, but he got it all wrong. He told the man, "The moon said to tell you that, just as every night I die, and dying perish, so you too will die, and perish utterly."

Any more to the story? Yes. When the moon heard this she was so mad with the rabbit that she hit him across the nose with a big stick. And to this day the rabbit has a slit in his nose where the moon hit him. And to this day mankind believes that when he dies he perishes utterly.

If you go look at a rabbit it does have a slit nose—and some would say that proves it's a true story. But the slit did not come from the moon! This is the storyteller's way of building in a memory device to get across his "deep truth." Every time someone saw a rabbit and looked at his funny, wriggly, slit nose, he might think, "That reminds me. I heard a story one time about death. Are we right to think we perish?"

Why tell funny stories about anything like dying? One reason is that we remember the funny ones, the ones called fables or myths, the ones with animals or good plots. And a story like this one is also about a very serious subject. It raises the question, "Why do we die?" Or, "Are we so sure that we die forever?"

Why do we die? Some blame death on the devil. We learned this in basic catechism. "Through the devil death entered the world." But a grownup way of putting this is necessary for grownups (perhaps even for children). Try this for adult size: the devil is the symbol of evil. And death is evil; it is part of the mystery of wickedness. To be a Christian is to believe that Jesus overcomes this evil.

The Hottentots in Africa are right to wonder if something is wrong in our thinking that death is the end. Everyone wonders, "Do we really go on living?" Remember the answer the moon gave that began, "Just as every night I die, and dying, rise." The real answer is not given by the moon. It is Jesus who died and rose. His rising is more a part of us than the return of spring each year, more than the rising of the sun each morning, more than the light that follows darkness. It is not the moon that sends us the message and gives us the word, but Jesus, and his Father. For their promise that we live, we give thanks. And for the life of our brother (sister) we give thanks, for that life which is God's gift and knows no ending.

DO NOT LIVE IN FEAR

Sometimes just a few words of Scripture turn on the light. They are not out of context; they stand out of the text, and for a blessed moment we are sure God is speaking. Take words like these, from the gospel of Luke: Jesus is talking with his followers and he says, "Do not live in fear, little flock. It has pleased your Father to give you the kingdom."

"Do not be afraid." "Do not live in fear." Many of us do. We live in fear of the future; what will tomorrow bring? It will bring the sun; it always has. If it brings the darkness we call death, it will also bring God. Our prophets and poets give many names to the future. Some call it heaven, or going home. Or the Great Supper, or paradise. The real name for our future is God.

There are fears we cannot banish, at least right away, with weapons of the Spirit—like the fear of losing one's job, or health, or savings. The fear of another war. The fear of accidents or misfortune coming to our children. What will tomorrow bring, or even today? We are right to be anxious about these things, and to provide as far as we can against them. When we pray in the liturgy to be delivered from anxiety it does not mean to ignore these concerns. It is a prayer that we be delivered from our deeper fears. These run very deep and can destroy us. There is the fear of being rejected and unwanted, the fear of being unknown, and unloved, and finally the fear of loss—the loss of friends and loved ones, the loss of life, theirs and our own, that we call death. Those other anxieties are shadows, but these fears are darkness. They are mountains that fall upon us, and we cry out, "Who will lift the stone?"

God says, "I will." For the fear of being unloved, we need to hear his voice saying, "With an everlasting love have I loved you. Can a mother forget the child of her womb? Even so, Israel, I will not forget you." Do people really believe this? Yes, they do, and believe it with an absolute assurance that may be the gift of faith but is also reinforced by wisdom.

One of the wisest teachers of our century, the great theologian Karl Barth, was asked once what was the most important truth he had ever learned. He answered by quoting the words of a childhood hymn, "Jesus loves me; this I know." Many of us have heard or sung that hymn. He believed it.

The fear of death is a darkness that makes children of us all, and we are not ashamed to call out when we are afraid. The whole point of believing is that there is someone there to answer. How is a child delivered from fear of the dark; is it by turning on the light? Some parents do turn on a lamp for a while, or leave a night-light burning. But this is a short-term solution. A child is really delivered from fear by his mother or father loving him—patting his head, soothing away bad dreams, tucking him in all over again. He is comforted and surrenders to sleep because he hears those famous words of reassurance, "It's all right." It is all right. The secret here is that all love—mother's, father's, the love we have for each other—is God's love; it is divine. And the meaning of Jesus' life is that such love is powerful. It is even powerful against death; it delivers us to life. We can surrender to that sleep in confidence, because he delivers us.

It is this power of love and reassurance that God gives us. Let us learn it now from the faith and love of each other, and the gift of God. Then we can relax with Jesus' words, "Do not live in fear, little flock. It has pleased your Father to give you the kingdom."

WHY DOES IT HAPPEN?

The following was written to a young couple, whose first child was stillborn:

You asked me how God could allow this to happen, especially since it has nothing to do with sin or moral failure.

Part of the answer is that the Creator did not make a perfect world. It is changing and evolving, and that means things going wrong; pain (and death itself) are part of it. The human person is such a complex and marvelous achievement, and the conception and birth of a new, unique personality is so astonishing that it should not surprise us if sometimes the process does not work.

You could well ask why the Creator chose to make an imperfect world in the first place. I can only suggest two answers but I think they are at the heart of the matter.

One is that, for believers, we live in a landscape that is larger than earth and time. And we live with the hope that our life is not bounded by death. You may find it hard to believe in eternal life, heaven, resurrection (or whatever term appeals to you). But there is no doubt that God promises this and Christ affirms it. It would be easier to believe in God's promises and to think those we love are alive—more alive than we are— if we stopped using our imagination (as the apostle Paul suggests). Our images of eternal life, including those of Scripture, are analogies, only shadows of the reality. It finally comes down to trust in God. And there is a common sense argument: would God make us only to destroy us in the end?

The second answer is that God has chosen to join us in this imperfect world and on our journey and by his presence, to help us get through it. The presence of God in human life goes by various names: spirit, grace, immanence, the Eternal Word, the risen Christ. It could be simply stated this way: we are not alone. The church has taught us this, and sacraments like baptism and holy communion help us to appreciate it or feel it. But reflecting on one's own experience can help us to see what they are talking about.

When difficult or tragic things happen, we surmount them. We have what theologians call the power to transcend them. And this power is not just from healthy living, or a good mental attitude. It is from God. Or the Holy Spirit in us. The second way we get through difficult times is with the help of our family and friends. Their love and concern and practical support mean very much. Scripture says, very simply, "Where love is, God is." It is this gift of love and compassion that we feel from others which is the presence of God.

I am not saying that God brings good out of evil, because that gives rise to the question of why there is evil in the first place (apart from the abuse of freedom). If you mean by evil such things in human life as pain, upset, suffering, and death, the two answers I have given are at least part of the answer. It is enough to carry us until God makes all things plain.

JTN

THE CUP OF LOVE

One time a young man in college faced the usual problem of students at Christmas—how to buy gifts with little money. He solved the problem, at least for his father, because the son's hobby was ceramics, and he did a pottery piece which he gift-wrapped and brought home. With it he enclosed this note:

> Here is a cup. I made it. I like it better than any-thing else I've ever made. Keep it for a while. Think of me when you drink from it. Someday, a long time from now, give it back to me. And I'll think of us when I drink from it.
>
> Love, John

Now let us reverse the roles—but not the love—a little. Picture a father, our heavenly Father, saying to a newborn child:

> Here is your life. I made it. I love you more than the trees and the oceans which I have also made. Keep your life for a time. Think of me as you live it. Someday, a long time from now, give it back to me. I will remember you, and you shall live.

There is simple beauty in John's words to his father. It reflects a deep love, and a knowledge that all things pass.

Even in the midst of life we know we are as the leaves that fall, the grass that perishes. But we are more than leaves or grass; we are persons. In this life we have chosen good over evil, preferred the light to darkness. And even when we have failed we have already experienced the divine mercy.

All love is one, all love is divine. Each time in this life that we have said, "I love you," or shown that love in deeds, we have been part of God. When the young college sophomore signed his Christmas note, "Love, John," one could have heard, with the ears to listen, the sound of angel wings. For this is a tiny moment of the presence of God.

At peace, then, we give our beloved back to God, the Giver of all good gifts. And we live with the confidence that love is stronger than death, and God's gift of life will continue.

READINGS

THE DESTINY
OF THE RIGHTEOUS

Wisdom 3:1-6, 9

But the souls of the righteous are
   in the hand of God,
and no torment will ever touch them.
In the eyes of the foolish they
   seemed to have died,
and their departure was thought to be a disaster,
and their going from us to be their destruction;
but they are at peace.
For though in the sight of others
   they were punished,
their hope is full of immortality.
Having been disciplined a little,
   they will receive great good,
because God tested them and
   found them worthy of himself;
like gold in the furnace he tried them....
Those who trust in him will understand truth,
and the faithful will abide with him in love,
because grace and mercy are upon his holy ones,
and he watches over his elect.

THE DIVINE SHEPHERD

Psalm 23

The Lord is my shepherd, I shall not want.
    He makes me lie down in green pastures;
he leads me beside still waters;
    he restores my soul.
He leads me in right paths
    for his name's sake.

Even though I walk through the darkest valley,
    I fear no evil;
for you are with me;
    your rod and your staff—
    they comfort me.

You prepare a table before me
    in the presence of my enemies;
you anoint my head with oil;
    my cup overflows.
Surely goodness and mercy shall follow me
    all the days of my life,
and I shall dwell in the house of the Lord
    my whole life long.

WAITING FOR
DIVINE REDEMPTION

Psalm 130

Out of the depths I cry to you, O Lord.
    Lord, hear my voice!
Let your ears be attentive
    to the voice of my supplications!

If you, O Lord, should mark iniquities,
    Lord, who could stand?
But there is forgiveness with you,
    so that you may be revered.

I wait for the Lord, my soul waits,
    and in his word I hope;
my soul waits for the Lord
    more than those who watch for the morning,
    more than those who watch for the morning.

O Israel, hope in the Lord!
    For with the Lord there is steadfast love,
    and with him is great power to redeem.
It is he who will redeem Israel
    from all its iniquities.

GOD'S LOVE
IN CHRIST JESUS

Romans 8:31b–35, 37–39

If God is for us, who is against us? He who did not withhold his own Son, but gave him up for all of us, will he not with him also give us everything else? Who will bring any charge against God's elect? It is God who justifies. Who is to condemn? It is Christ Jesus, who died, yes, who was raised, who is at the right hand of God, who indeed intercedes for us.

Who will separate us from the love of Christ? Will hardship, or distress, or persecution, or famine, or nakedness, or peril, or sword? No, in all these things we are more than conquerors through him who loved us. For I am convinced that neither death, nor life, nor angels, nor rulers, nor things present, nor things to come, nor powers, nor height, nor depth, nor anything else in all creation, will be able to separate us from the love of God in Christ Jesus our Lord.

LIVING BY FAITH

2 Corinthians 5:1, 6–10

For we know that if the earthly tent we live in is destroyed, we have a building from God, a house not made with hands, eternal in the heavens.

So we are always confident; even though we know that while we are at home in the body we are away from the Lord—for we walk by faith, not by sight. Yes, we do have confidence, and we would rather be away from the body and at home with the Lord. So whether we are at home or away, we make it our aim to please him. For all of us must appear before the judgment seat of Christ, so that each may receive recompense for what has been done in the body, whether good or evil.

THERE WILL BE
NO MORE DEATH

Revelation 21:1–5a, 6b–7

Then I saw a new heaven and a new earth; for the first heaven and the first earth had passed away, and the sea was no more. And I saw the holy city, the new Jerusalem, coming down out of heaven from God, prepared as a bride adorned for her husband. And I heard a loud voice from the throne saying, "See, the home of God is among mortals. He will dwell with them; they will be his peoples, and God himself will be with them. He will wipe every tear from their eyes. Death will be no more; mourning and crying and pain will be no more, for the first things have passed away."

And the one who was seated on the throne said, "See, I am making all things new. I am the Alpha and the Omega, the beginning and the end. To the thirsty I will give water as a gift from the spring of the water of life. Those who conquer will inherit these things, and I will be their God and they will be my children."

THE BEATITUDES

Matthew 5:1–12a

When Jesus saw the crowds, he went up the mountain; and after he sat down, his disciples came to him. Then he began to speak, and taught them, saying: "Blessed are the poor in spirit,
for theirs is the kingdom of heaven.
Blessed are those who mourn,
for they will be comforted.
Blessed are the meek,
for they will inherit the earth.
Blessed are those who hunger and thirst for righteousness,
for they will be filled.
Blessed are the merciful,
for they will receive mercy.
Blessed are the pure in heart,
for they will see God.
Blessed are the peacemakers,
for they will be called children of God.
Blessed are those who are persecuted for righteousness' sake,
for theirs is the kingdom of heaven.
Blessed are you when people revile you and persecute you and utter all kinds of evil against you falsely on my account. Rejoice and be glad, for your reward is great in heaven."

COME TO ME...AND I WILL GIVE YOU REST

Matthew 11:25–30

At that time Jesus said, "I thank you, Father, Lord of heaven and earth, because you have hidden these things from the wise and the intelligent and have revealed them to infants; yes, Father, for such was your gracious will. All things have been handed over to me by my Father; and no one knows the Son except the Father, and no one knows the Father except the Son and anyone to whom the Son chooses to reveal him.

"Come to me, all you that are weary and are carrying heavy burdens, and I will give you rest. Take my yoke upon you, and learn from me; for I am gentle and humble in heart, and you will find rest for your souls. For my yoke is easy, and my burden is light."

COME, YOU WHOM MY FATHER HAS BLESSED

Matthew 25:31–40

"When the Son of Man comes in his glory, and all the angels with him, then he will sit on the throne of his glory. All the nations will be gathered before him, and he will separate people one from another as a shepherd separates the sheep from the goats, and he will put the sheep at his right hand and the goats at the left. Then the king will say to those at his right hand, 'Come, you that are blessed by my Father, inherit the kingdom prepared for you from the foundation of the world; for I was hungry and you gave me food, I was thirsty and you gave me something to drink, I was a stranger and you welcomed me, I was naked and you gave me clothing, I was sick and you took care of me, I was in prison and you visited me.' Then the righteous will answer him, 'Lord, when was it that we saw you hungry and gave you food, or thirsty and gave you something to drink? And when was it that we saw you a stranger and welcomed you, or naked and gave you clothing? And when was it that we saw you sick or in prison and visited you?' And the king will answer them, 'Truly I tell you, just as you did it to one of the least of these who are members of my family, you did it to me.'"

THE WALK TO EMMAUS

Luke 24:13–16, 28–35

Now on that same day two of them were going to a village called Emmaus, about seven miles from Jerusalem, and talking with each other about all these things that had happened. While they were talking and discussing, Jesus himself came near and went with them, but their eyes were kept from recognizing him....

As they came near the village to which they were going, he walked ahead as if he were going on. But they urged him strongly, saying, "Stay with us, because it is almost evening and the day is now nearly over." So he went in to stay with them.

When he was at the table with them, he took the bread, blessed and broke it, and gave it to them. Then their eyes were opened, and they recognized him; and he vanished from their sight. They said to each other, "Were not our hearts burning within us while he was talking to us on the road, while he was opening the scriptures to us?" That same hour they got up and returned to Jerusalem; and they found the eleven and their companions gathered together. They were saying, "The Lord has risen indeed, and he has appeared to Simon!" Then they told what had happened on the road, and how he had been made known to them in the breaking of the bread.

THE RESURRECTION AND THE LIFE

John 11:17–27

When Jesus arrived, he found that Lazarus had already been in the tomb four days. Now Bethany was near Jerusalem, some two miles away, and many of the Jews had come to Martha and Mary to console them about their brother. When Martha heard that Jesus was coming, she went and met him, while Mary stayed at home. Martha said to Jesus, "Lord, if you had been here, my brother would not have died. But even now I know that God will give you whatever you ask of him." Jesus said to her, "Your brother will rise again." Martha said to him, "I know that he will rise again in the resurrection on the last day." Jesus said to her, "I am the resurrection and the life. Those who believe in me, even though they die, will live, and everyone who lives and believes in me will never die. Do you believe this?" She said to him, "Yes, Lord, I believe that you are the Messiah, the Son of God, the one coming into the world."

MAGDALENE

John 20:11–18

Mary stood weeping outside the tomb. As she wept, she bent over to look into the tomb; and she saw two angels in white, sitting where the body of Jesus had been lying, one at the head and the other at the feet. They said to her, "Woman, why are you weeping?" She said to them, "They have taken away my Lord, and I do not know where they have laid him." When she had said this, she turned around and saw Jesus standing there, but she did not know that it was Jesus. Jesus said to her, "Woman, why are you weeping? Whom are you looking for?" Supposing him to be the gardener, she said to him, "Sir, if you have carried him away, tell me where you have laid him, and I will take him away." Jesus said to her, "Mary!" She turned and said to him in Hebrew, "Rabbouni!" (which means Teacher). Jesus said to her, "Do not hold on to me, because I have not yet ascended to the Father. But go to my brothers and say to them, 'I am ascending to my Father and your Father, to my God and your God.'" Mary Magdalene went and announced to the disciples, "I have seen the Lord"; and she told them that he had said these things to her.

JESUS AND THOMAS

John 20:24–30

Thomas (who was called the Twin), one of the twelve, was not with them when Jesus came. So the other disciples told him, "We have seen the Lord." But he said to them, "Unless I see the mark of the nails in his hands, and put my finger in the mark of the nails and my hand in his side, I will not believe."

A week later his disciples were again in the house, and Thomas was with them. Although the doors were shut, Jesus came and stood among them and said, "Peace be with you." Then he said to Thomas, "Put your finger here and see my hands. Reach out your hand and put it in my side. Do not doubt but believe." Thomas answered him, "My Lord and my God!" Jesus said to him, "Have you believed because you have seen me? Blessed are those who have not seen and yet have come to believe."

Now Jesus did many other signs in the presence of his disciples, which are not written in this book. But these are written so that you may come to believe that Jesus is the Messiah, the Son of God, and that through believing you may have life in his name.

JESUS APPEARS
TO SEVEN DISCIPLES

John 21:1–14

After these things Jesus showed himself again to the disciples by the Sea of Tiberias; and he showed himself in this way. Gathered there together were Simon Peter, Thomas called the Twin, Nathanael of Cana in Galilee, the sons of Zebedee, and two others of his disciples. Simon Peter said to them, "I am going fishing." They said to him, "We will go with you." They went out and got into the boat, but that night they caught nothing.

Just after daybreak, Jesus stood on the beach; but the disciples did not know that it was Jesus. Jesus said to them, "Children, you have no fish, have you?" They answered him, "No." He said to them, "Cast the net to the right side of the boat, and you will find some." So they cast it, and now they were not able to haul it in because there were so many fish. That disciple whom Jesus loved said to Peter, "It is the Lord!" When Simon Peter heard that it was the Lord, he put on some clothes, for he was naked, and jumped into the sea. But the other disciples came in the boat, dragging the net full of fish, for they were not far from the land, only about a hundred yards off.

When they had gone ashore, they saw a charcoal fire there, with fish on it, and bread. Jesus said to them, "Bring some of the fish that you have just caught." So Simon Peter went aboard and hauled the net ashore, full of large fish, a hundred fifty-three of them; and though there were so many, the net was not torn. Jesus said to them, "Come and have breakfast." Now none of the disciples dared to ask him, "Who are you?" because they knew it was the Lord. Jesus came and took the bread and gave it to them, and did the same with the fish. This was now the third time that Jesus appeared to the disciples after he was raised from the dead.

THE HEAVENLY BANQUET

Adapted from verses in Isaiah

Come to the feast.
I have made the earth a garden
of flowers and delights,
of rich foods and choice wines.
The grape is pressed,
the harvest gathered.
Call in the friend, the passerby.
Find the forgotten, the friendless.
Let there be no sorrow, no weeping.
Come in to my feast!

You with the weapon, put it down.
You with the clenched fist, open it.
There is a veil over your eyes.
I will remove it.
It has kept you from seeing
that you are all my children,
that I have desired you,
in all your variety,
to be the bride of my son.

Come, then, all you
begotten of my love.
My house is open,
the table spread.
The bridegroom waits.

Based on Revelation 22:13, 16–17, 20

"I am Alpha and the Omega,
the beginning of all things
    and their end,
He who is,
    and was,
    and still to come:
the Almighty.

Patience, I am coming soon!
And with me comes the award I make,
repaying each one according
    to the life they have lived.

I, Jesus, have sent my angel
    to give you the assurance of this
    in your churches;
I, the root,
I, the offspring of David's race,
I, the bright star
 that ushers in the morning.

The Spirit and my Bride bid me come;
let everyone who hears this read aloud,
    say 'Come!'
Come, you who are thirsty,
    take, you who will, the water of life;
    it is my free gift."

Be it so, then;
    come, Lord Jesus.

ODE TO A CAPABLE WIFE (OR, THE VALIANT WOMAN)

Proverbs 31:10–31

A capable wife who can find?
    She is far more precious than jewels.
The heart of her husband trusts in her,
    and he will have no lack of gain.
She does him good, and not harm,
    all the days of her life.
She seeks wool and flax,
    and works with willing hands.
She is like the ships of the merchant,
    she brings her food from far away.
She rises while it is still night
    and provides food for her household
    and tasks for her servant-girls.
She considers a field and buys it;
    with the fruit of her hands she plants a vineyard.
She girds herself with strength,
    and makes her arms strong.
She perceives that her merchandise is profitable.
    Her lamp does not go out at night.
She puts her hands to the distaff,
    and her hands hold the spindle.
She opens her hand to the poor,

and reaches out her hands to the needy.
She is not afraid for her household when it snows,
    for all her household are clothed in crimson.
She makes herself coverings;
    her clothing is fine linen and purple.
Her husband is known in the city gates,
    taking his seat among the elders of the land.
She makes linen garments and sells them;
    she supplies the merchant with sashes.
Strength and dignity are her clothing,
    and she laughs at the time to come.
She opens her mouth with wisdom,
    and the teaching of kindness is on her tongue.
She looks well to the ways of her household,
    and does not eat the bread of idleness.
Her children rise up and call her happy;
    her husband too, and he praises her:
"Many women have done excellently,
    but you surpass them all."
Charm is deceitful, and beauty is vain,
    but a woman who fears the Lord is to be praised.
Give her a share in the fruit of her hands,
    and let her works praise her in the city gates.

PRAYERS

O God with whom there is no death,
we pray to you for our beloved,
for those who shared life with us
and have finished their journey.
We believe, it is our faith,
that the grave does not contain them
or mark their final resting place.

O God of compassion,
forgive whatever their failings
and bring them home at last.
You made them, you loved them,
and in your will is our peace.

Lord of life and lover
of all that you have made,
we pray to you in the midst of death
that you raise us up
beyond our sorrows and our fears.

Help us to believe
what no mortal eye can see,
that beyond the boundaries of our sight
is another land and richer life
which you prepare for us.
Unite us,
beyond all pain and separation,
with those we have loved,
and yourself.

Father who begot us,
we pray you for ourselves
living in the midst of death,
dying in the midst of life.
Deliver us from the last aloneness
and send us that most sweet companion
whom we have learned to call Jesus,
the way, the truth, and the life.

Lord of all life,
we pray to you in the midst of life
for those who die,
that you may be their shelter
and heaven their home.

We give you those who made us and loved
us,
who befriended and cherished us,
and we await with confidence
the day of reunion,
for we are all the children of your love.
Maker of worlds
and parent of the living,
we turn to you
because there is nowhere else to go.
Our wisdom does not hold us
and all our strength
is weakness in the end.

O Lord who made us
and sent prophets and Jesus to teach us,
help us to hear, to understand
that in your word there is life.

Maker of man and woman
and taker of what you have made,
do not let us fear death
if Jesus has won the victory
and we are his brothers and sisters
in the spirit and of the flesh.

Help us to be like your Son
who dying still called you Father
and found in your love
the place of surrender.

By the word we hear
and the bread we share
give us your strength.
We bear about in our bodies
not the mark of the nails
but the seeds of our own dissolution.

Our dying is written
on the face of our flesh.
It is our share
in the cross of our Lord Jesus Christ.
We do not boast of it
but of his victory.

Let no man trouble us.
If we know his dying
we will also know his rising.
If we drink his cup
it is not only sorrow we share
but the cup of joy.

"All that matters
is that one is created anew."

My brothers and sisters,
we are the children of God
who has delivered us to life.
Let us not fear death, then,
for it is but the sleep
from which he awakens us.

We are the seed that dies
and comes to life
and bears much fruit.

Let not the time of departure
fill us with dread
for we have one who has taught us to pray
"Father, into your hands
I commend my spirit."

Let us not be fearful of our dying
for we are not alone.
There is one we have known
in the breaking of the bread
and he is still our companion.

We hear his voice; he tells us,
"My name is Jesus, and I live."

The following prayer was written for Jane, who died at 18. It is especially fitting for the funeral or memorial of any young person.

Jesus grew older,
he never grew old.
He died young.
He rose young.
A melody in the night
still sung.
A tale in the evening
still told.

O beautiful One,
undying One!
Finish in joy
what love has begun.
Lead us beyond the trying,
the living, the dying.
Make us new again.
And young.
Forever young.

May he support us all the day long,
until the shadows lengthen
and the evening comes
and the busy world is hushed
and the fever of life is over
and our work is done!
Then in his mercy
may he grant us a safe lodging
and a holy rest
and peace at the last.

John Henry Newman

Let nothing disturb thee,
Nothing affright thee;
All things are passing;
God never changes.
Patient endurance
Attains to all things;
The one God possesses
In nothing is wanting;
God alone suffices.

St. Teresa of Avila

Watch thou, dear Lord,
with those who wake,
or watch,
or weep tonight,
and give thine angels and saints charge
over those who sleep.
Tend thy sick ones, O Lord Christ,
rest thy weary ones,
bless thy dying ones,
pity thine afflicted ones,
and all for thy love's sake!

St. Augustine

A SONG OF JOY
(AND PREFACE FOR EASTER)

O God of earth and sky and all that live,
not thanks alone we give
but make the universe a song of praise
for this most excellent of days
when Jesus Christ is risen, Lord on high,
inviting us to live, and bidding death to die.

We too have pain and sorrow known
but know at last his story: we are not alone.
In that dark passage he has gone before,
unbarred the gate, flung wide the door
to life, to life! and love's embrace.

Upon this glorious day the night shall not
descend,
nor shadows end the light of glory on his face.
Jesus, savior, friend and kin
who wore our flesh and bore our sin —
he lives! The angels sing. Creation gives
 a shout of Alleluia, God be praised
for Jesus Christ, and Easter days!

JTN

As the rain hides the stars,
as the autumn mist hides the hills,
as the clouds veil the blue of the sky,
so the dark happenings of my life hide
the shining of Thy face from me.
Yet if I may hold Thy hand in the darkness,
it is enough.
Even though I may stumble in my going,
Thou dost not fall. Thou dost not fall.

An old Gaelic prayer

DIVINE PROVIDENCE

GOD HAS CREATED ME
to do Him some definite service
He has committed some work to me
which He has not committed to another

I HAVE MY MISSION
I may never know it in this life
but I shall be told it in the next

I AM A LINK IN A CHAIN
a bond of connection between persons
He has not created me for naught
I shall do good—I shall do His work
I shall be an angel of peace
a preacher of truth in my own place
while not intending it
if I do but keep His commandments

THEREFORE I WILL TRUST HIM
whatever I am, I can never be thrown away
If I am in sickness, my sickness may serve Him
in perplexity, my perplexity may serve Him
If I am in sorrow, my sorrow may serve Him

HE DOES NOTHING IN VAIN
He knows what He is about
He may take away my friends
He may throw me among strangers
He may make me feel desolate
make my spirits sink
hide my future from me—still

HE KNOWS WHAT HE IS ABOUT

John Henry Newman

PRAYER OF HOPE
AT TIME OF DEATH

God of creation, on the first day of life
you set our feet on a journey toward death
and each day hurries us on;
day and night pass and there is no return.
Did you make us only to grow old
and fall like the leaves that die,
that return to dust and are no more?
We cannot believe this but we need your help.
Alone of all your creatures we ask these questions.
No star cries out in pain,
the lion and the trees do not weep,
the birds have no song of mourning.
By the gift you have given us to know ourselves
and to know we are mortal,
help us also to know you, the immortal, the
undying One.
Confirm our hope
that we are made in your image
and there is that in us which cannot die.
Let not the deed of your creation
return to chaos and darkness.
We are your glory!
We alone of all creatures
have raised our heads and walked the earth.

We alone have made songs and drawn pictures
and died for goodness and tried to love.
O thou eternal and abiding One!
Do not abandon the work of your hands.

JTN

CONFESSION OF SINS

This prayer is fitting for a general confession at any point in life, and also when life is ending. It has been used with penitents at certain times to give them sacramental absolution—the assurance of God's forgiveness for their sins.

O God, I ask your pardon for my sins—
for any acts of malice or meanness
in my entire life.
I ask you to forgive me
for any misuse I have made
of the gift of speech,
the gift of my sexuality,
for the gift of time, and of life itself.

I ask your pardon for my forgotten sins,
for anything I have ever done to hurt others,
and to hurt myself.
I would like to be an unselfish
and giving person,
a more loving and forgiving person.
Your son Jesus spoke so often of your kingdom,
the coming of justice, peace, and love
in human life.
Let me be part of it.

Help me by your grace
not only to repent my sins
but to live my baptism,
to be faithful to my promises.

I come to you in trust and confidence
because your prophets declared
you are the God of compassion,
slow to anger,
ever ready to forgive,
and your son Jesus taught us to think of you
as a loving Father,
who welcomes us home.

I know that Jesus taught us
a new commandment:
to love you with all my heart and soul,
with all my mind and strength,
and to love my neighbor as myself.
I confess once more
the times I have failed to do so,
and I ask the help of the Holy Spirit
to make my life pleasing in your sight.
AMEN.

RITUALS

The most widely watched funeral in the world, of Diana, Princess of Wales, gave testimony to the power of ritual. This was a specially arranged service that combined many of the best features with which we honor the dead, such as: procession, a church of great beauty, music (of many kinds), a superb choir and great organ, involvement of the people, and the eloquence of the spoken word. The intercessions, called Prayers of the People, were delivered with great clarity and calm by the Archbishop. The Prime Minister read the Scripture readings so well that some listeners, unfamiliar with the Bible, spoke of his ability to compose a great speech!

In one way or another, we should use rituals and symbols; it is the way meaning lays hold of us, a sense of mystery and transcendence that believers simply call the presence of God. A service in a funeral home may also use Scripture readings, poetry, a sermon or eulogy, prayer, music and hymns. The readings in prayers in this book may be helpful, and a choice from the Reflections could be used as another reading, or incorporated into a sermon.

Services in church follow the ritual books of the church, but still allow for participation. Here are a suggested opening prayer, a model of the General Intercessions (which may be composed new for each service), two prayers of commendation, and suggestions for the brief ritual at the grave.

OPENING PRAYER

Let us pray...

> Loving God,
> we pray you on behalf of your servant____
> and all who die in faith,
> that you may welcome them to your dwelling place
> with the saints and angels,
> and those who have gone before us.
> Comfort the living; sustain us in this time of sorrow.
> We pray in the name of Jesus our brother,
> who shared our life and death
> and enables us to live with hope—
> he who lives and reigns with you as God,
> for ever and ever.

Reading of the Scriptures and a homily (sermon) follow. At some point in the service (in the Catholic rite it is always after the Scriptures and homily) the prayer called the General Intercessions may be used, led perhaps by one of the family or mourners. The people may be invited to make the response to each petition ("Lord, hear our prayer"). Additional petitions and specific names may be added.

GENERAL INTERCESSIONS

Father of mercies and God of all consolation,
we pray in compassion for each other,
and seeking your help:

For our families and friends,
for all those who grieve,
that they may be comforted,
let us pray to the Lord...
Lord, hear our prayer.

In loving memory of_____.
For all those who have left us for a time,
that they may know the joy of your presence,
let us pray to the Lord...
Lord, hear our prayer.

For ourselves, that faith may sustain us,
the memory of our love be dear to us,
and the hope of resurrection be strong in us,
let us pray to the Lord...
Lord, hear our prayer.

For those who are suffering at this hour,
and for those who minister to them,
and for the dying, that they may be at peace,
let us pray to the Lord...
Lord, hear our prayer.

For all who ever gave us life, and love,
and the labor of their hands and hearts,
who helped us and made us,
let us pray to the Lord...
Lord, hear our prayer.

O God with whom there is no death,
we give you thanks for the life of_____
and ask you to reunite us in eternal life,
through Jesus Christ, our Lord...
Amen.

If Eucharist follows (as it does in the Roman Catholic Mass of Christian Burial) the gifts of bread and wine are brought up, by members of the family or friends. Sometimes tokens of a person's life are included (or they are placed on the casket), such as a Bible, or a cross, or a crucifix. Music or hymns are fitting at this time, and at communion. The body of the deceased is always honored, sometimes with incense, which suggests that the offering of the person's life to God is now complete. The service may conclude with either of the following Prayers of Commendation.

A PRAYER
OF COMMENDATION (1)

Go forth O Christian soul
    in the name of God who made you,
    in the name of God who redeemed you
    in the name of God who sanctifies you.
Go forth in the name of the triune God
    whose names you said in life,
    whose child you are.
Love that created you, receive her (him) now.
Love that sustained you, receive her (him) now.
Love that sanctified you, receive her (him) now.
O God of the living
    fountain and source of all life,
    take your servant from the trials of this life
    to the place of blessedness where you abide.
May Jesus, who knew suffering and death,
    be her (his) companion,
    her (his) good shepherd in this dark valley.
May the angels and saints pray for her (him),
    the blessed Joseph, patron of the dying,
    pray for her (him),
    the virgin Mary, who stood at the cross,
    pray for her (him),
    and may they receive her (him)
    in the life beyond life,

the blessed eternity that Jesus promised.
When he was among us, he told his disciples,
"I go to prepare a place for you,
    that where I am, you also may be."
O loving and merciful God,
    receive your own daughter (son),
        the one created and nourished by your love.

A PRAYER
OF COMMENDATION (2)

Father who made us, unto your mercy which is beyond all telling, and unto your love which is the last good answer to the deepest longing of our hearts, we commend the life of your servant_____who has left us, for a time but not forever. We ask you to hear our prayer on his (her) behalf as we speak in sorrow but also in faith. Lord our God, may he (she) who used your gift of life to share it with others now enter upon the more abundant life that Jesus promised. May he (she) who bore witness to your love and faithfulness, your truth and goodness, now enter upon the reward that is promised the just one and share the victory of our brother Jesus Christ. Bring him (her), Lord, to the light that will never know darkness, to the joy that will never weary or cease to delight, to the fullness and possession of all those good things with which you blessed him (her) in life.

Forgive any weakness which may have been a sign of human frailty, and accept him (her) as one of the joyous company redeemed by Jesus Christ. Admit him (her) to the joy of which the Holy Spirit said, "Eye has not seen, nor ear heard, nor has it entered the heart of man to know, the things the Father has prepared for those who love him."

O Lord our God, may he (she) who persevered in the faith now enter upon the Kingdom. May your servant, who gave us his (her) life and labor and love find a place at the banquet where you are the bridegroom and we are your beloved. We give to you, in Christian faith and human sorrow, the one you gave to us, the one we have been glad to know as (...husband and father, son and brother, companion and friend, etc....). We thank you for the gift of his (her) life. And with your help we believe that his (her) life continues and we shall see him (her) again.

THE BURIAL

At the place of burial, the service should be brief. Suggested: the prayer for blessing or hallowing of the grave, an invitation to join hands and say the Lord's Prayer, and a final prayer and blessing. It is also helpful, instead of handing out copies, to ask people to repeat, line by line, the words of the Good Shepherd psalm, or the Prayer of Commendation (1) or the greatly esteemed prayer by Bede Jarrett ("We give them back to you, O Lord"). If a worship folder (program) has been handed out in church, one of these prayers may be printed on the back cover; it is useful for meditation while people wait, and can be used at the grave.

The invitation, often given, to share a meal afterwards (which many churches provide) is not only hospitable but a small reflection of the Great Supper or heavenly banquet which the beloved now enjoys. For the living it becomes a time of reunion, and remembrance of happy things in the past.

Blessing at the Grave

> Creator God,
> You made us from the dust of the earth
>   and breathed into us the gift of life.
> Bless, hallow, make holy this earth
>   to which we now return the body of our beloved.
> Confirm our faith that his (her) life continues,
>   a gift that we return to You.

WE GIVE THEM BACK

We give them back to you, O Lord,
who first gave them to us,
and as you did not lose them in the giving
so we do not lose them in the return.
Not as the world gives do you give,
O Lover of souls!
For what is yours is ours also,
if we belong to you!
Life is unending because love is undying,
and the boundaries of this mortal life
are but an horizon,
and an horizon is but the limit of our sight.
Lift us up, strong Son of God,
that we may see further!
Strengthen us in faith, that we may see
beyond the horizon!
And while you prepare a place for us,
as you have promised,
prepare us also for that happy place,
that where you are we may be also,
with those we have loved, forever.

Bede Jarrett, O.P.

POSTSCRIPT—
PRACTICAL DETAILS

This is very much a postscript because my hope is that readers will spend time in prayer and reflection on the preceding material. But when the text was done I felt that I should share some practical suggestions that come from much observation and participation in funerals.

Customs

How we approach our own death or the deaths of those we know and love should make a difference. I am not speaking here of widow's weeds or black armbands or extended mourning, but the customs of some peoples should be continued or adapted. It was once customary to place a wreath of mourning on the door (just as some Italian families place a spray of flowers to announce a birth). For some it is appropriate during the interval to the funeral to turn off the ever-present TV, radio (and now, the computer). The concerned pastor visits the family immediately in the home where they are gathering and leads them in prayer (for Catholics, the rosary is very apt).

We need ritual prayers, memorized, to say easily from the heart. Think of the traditional Catholic refrain, often recited at the grave: "Eternal rest grant unto them, O Lord." And the response: "And let perpetual light shine upon them." "May they rest in peace." "Amen." "May their souls and the souls of all the faithful departed through the mercy of God rest in peace." "Amen."

Think of the Jewish practice of *kaddish*, faithfully recited by devout Jews in memory of their dead. Flowers and candles have their place, of course, but we need words that are easily spoken, and sung.

Preparation

A most useful item I can think of at the time of death is a complete telephone list of people to be notified. For the most part, someone else should make the calls. You may wish to call the closest family members yourself, but by all means share the larger list. It spares you the pain of endlessly repeating details. When friends ask, "What can I do," give them something to do. And first of all, offer to make the calls for them ("I'm calling for so and so. It's sad news. He wants you to know, etc."). I repeat (from experience): this is a very great help.

Wishes of the Deceased

There is a point where some people are willing to talk about their death, and to make specific requests for their funeral (such as the wish for an open or closed casket, having a wake service or not, etc.). Some churches even have forms that the living make out in advance; others think the funeral rites are for the living, and this approach is too restrictive. One needs some balance here. Certainly people with good musical taste do not want certain types of music or hymns used for their last time in church. Others have favorite passages of Scripture or poetry they would like to be used.

Memorial Cards
Funeral directors usually provide these for everyone but the art and sentiment are better chosen by a family member, and the funeral director will assist with a quick printing.

Plan ahead. Find a Scripture quotation, a line of verse, perhaps a picture, whatever seems appropriate. Something more than name, date of birth, date of death. Some examples: St. Thomas More's great line, "Pray for me, as I will for thee, till we merrily meet in heaven," or, a single line from T.S. Eliot with the etching of a sailing ship: "Not farewell, traveler, fare forward." On the reverse side, the verse from John's gospel: "Jesus was standing on the shore" (John 21:4). Or this passage from St. Augustine: "There we shall rest, and we shall see; we shall see, and we shall love; we shall love and we shall praise. Behold what shall be in the end without end." To repeat: memorial cards are often misfitted to the person and the family tastes because no one takes thought in advance.

Worship Folder (Program)
More and more these are prepared for both weddings and funerals, setting out the order of worship, the hymns (at least the words, the music if possible—permissions may be necessary), perhaps a message from the family, a picture, some fitting art. Like memorial cards, this is difficult to prepare in a short time, but it personalizes and enhances the rite. And also it is a great aid for people in praying and singing together. So, do it, and ask for help. Some parishes

have a handsomely styled folder ready to go, needing only names and hymn titles.

Participation in the Service

Even in the most formal churches it is now customary or expected that people will volunteer or be selected by the family to do one or more Scripture readings, etc. In the Catholic Mass of Christian Burial, provision is made for laypeople to do the first two Scripture readings (such as those presented in this book). The gospel is always given by the deacon or priest. Laypeople also lead the Prayer of the Faithful, bring up the gifts, and if necessary assist at communion.

Readings should be well done, and, if possible, rehearsed at the microphone. Some obvious pointers which are often ignored: speak close to a microphone, speak slowly, distinctly, especially with consonants, the ending of words. But not so slow that it sounds exaggerated. To speak thoughtfully is perhaps the best way to put it. When there are few to mourn, and no volunteers, some parishes have enough forethought to provide one or two retired people for every funeral who are capable of reading the Scriptures. The service should not be dominated by a soloist or minister or priest.

A Memorial or Thanksgiving

The word "eulogy" is not ideal, but frequently used. Instead, arrange for someone to speak in remembrance or thanksgiving. This is now an accepted practice, including the liturgical churches, and usually occurs toward the end. It should follow certain guidelines. Usually there should be no more than one or two persons (funerals of outstanding people often go beyond this). The message should be relatively short. Avoid giving another sermon. It is the task of the clergyman to build faith, it is the privilege of this speaker to recall a person's life, to do so gratefully and with style. Be anecdotal, specific. Sketch briefly the biography; don't assume everyone present knows all the facts of birth, growing up, education, marriage, children, etc. Just recapitulate them briefly and then highlight the interesting things you know or find out about the deceased. Write out the text, typed if possible ("speaking from the heart" is often a disaster). A typed text can be taken over by someone else if a family member has difficulty with it.

If many people want to speak, suggest (or insist) that this be done at the wake service. And indeed, in one church where the wake is carried out in the church the night before, with the body present, the entire congregation was asked to contribute reminiscences of a beloved teacher and friend. It was a wonderful time, more filled with laughter than tears. Too many people speaking at the church service unbalances the whole ritual. On the other hand, some people's lives are very rich, and worthy of much recall.

Hospitality
People ask to help, and you should take them at their word. When Martin Luther King was murdered, Robert Kennedy made that offer, and Mrs. King asked him to provide a private plane. He did. Ask people to provide meals and lodging and transportation. And remember to volunteer yourself.

Some churches provide the parish hall and a meal after the funeral. Some are organized into guilds who take turns providing all these things. That is true of an early parish where I served, and in the best sense they took over when a woman died who had just moved into the parish. Her husband was not a Catholic, they had no children, and knew no one. He was so moved by the hospitality and practical help of people who were technically strangers that he joined the church and parish. "By this sign you shall know them."

Scheduling a Wake

Here are some warnings: if you decide upon two days, both afternoon and evening, you will likely be exhausted by running around, with little food and sleep. Choose the minimum time possible to meet people and share their company and sympathy.

Attitudes toward a wake service vary widely, and the choice is strictly up to you, the survivors (including an open or closed casket). Catholic wakes began as socializing, then moved to a rosary (or many rosaries) and now, quite often a combination of Scripture readings and two or three decades of the rosary. If the latter is done, it must be scheduled at the start of the wake; otherwise, it is sometimes impossible to assemble the people. In many places people choose to attend the wake service instead of the funeral, which is regrettable.

Time

For morning funerals, avoid too early an hour (such as 9:00). People are too tired. If meals are to follow, 10 or 11 is usually a fitting time. Customs are beginning to vary widely here. Some prefer an evening service (such as the Catholic Mass) with the burial the next day or a few days later reserved strictly for the family. Another approach is to have the burial and follow up within a month's time with the funeral Mass when all can gather.

One much loved physician I knew (Dr. Frank Drinan) specified an evening Mass with everyone invited to hospitality in the parish hall. The argument for evening is that more can come; on the other hand, many employers allow bereavement time. And evening funerals are sometimes hard to accommodate with a busy parish schedule.

Remembering

The older Catholic custom of "a month's mind Mass" (thirty days later), and an annual Mass on or near the date of death should be maintained. I have seen it bring together relatives who rarely meet (or go to church), but who honor a deceased parent every year. It also provides a little church-going, and a priest can make a warm contact with them.

The praying of the dead out of purgatory is fading from Catholic consciousness. But remembering the dead in gratitude should not fade. There has been a decided shift from deep mourning to quiet acceptance of death and confidence in the resurrection. Typical is the shift from black vestments to white, and the disappearance of the tallow candles. But some think it has gone too far; there should be a place for mourning. The old *Dies irae* will not appeal to many, but others object to a high note of celebration. Death remains a wound of love. It is healed not just by time, but by rituals, and ultimately, by the grace of friends and God.

Music

If people don't readily sing, be sure to employ a cantor and soloist; their fees, and the fee of the organist, are fully deserved (funeral directors usually take care of this). There is room for individual choice here, a very wide choice, but one that still should meet church approval. A favorite Taizé chant, easily sung, is "Lord, remember me when you come into your kingdom." There are some perennial good hymns such as "O God Our Help In Ages Past." And, of course, hymns of Easter and the resurrection.

A favorite with many (for both weddings and funerals) is the lovely Irish hymn, "Lord of All Hopefulness." For others, "On Eagle's Wings" remains the favorite, and Sister Suzanne Toolan's "I Am the Bread of Life." Liturgical Press publishes a helpful booklet, *The Order of Christian Funerals: Music for the Rite.* For a classical taste it is difficult to surpass the two great Handel pieces from the *Messiah,* "I Know That My Redeemer Liveth," and "Behold, I Tell You a Mystery." Bach at his best is represented by "Jesu, Joy of Man's Desiring" and "Sheep May Safely Graze." There are also many others from his great repertoire.

A French (or French Canadian) funeral echoes the lovely "J'irai La Voir un Jour," and Hispanic Catholics have shared with us "Pescadores des Hombres." For patriotic music, the national anthem is not fitting, but "America the Beautiful" is. To cover the coffin with the flag when the body is in church is often not permitted; instead, a white cloth (the pall) with religious symbols is used, to call to mind the person's baptism. But military rites, especially at the grave, have their place; they are a ritual that expresses great dignity and care.

Cremation

It is now accepted by most churches, and there is some need to integrate it into a church service. Secular rites memorialize the person and perhaps use some poetry, and music. Anyone who saw the prize-winning Czech film *Kolya* knows that, while classical music may be well done, the ritual at the crematory can appear painfully lacking. In the church, there is no reason not to have the urn containing the ashes placed where the casket is usually put. The Roman Catholic church prefers to have the body present (and the cremation afterward), but this is not always practical. A picture of the deceased is often displayed. To repeat: cremation is a valid choice, often dictated by circumstances. In a profound sense, it does not matter to those who believe in the resurrection but many will still prefer to honor the body as in the past.

Pallbearers

Wherever possible let this service be done by family or friends. There is something wrong or at least lacking when there are what are called "professional pallbearers." Sons and daughters, nephews, nieces, grandchildren, cousins, friends should offer this last service—and not as "honorary" assistance.

An Italian bishop one time, on a lonely road in his small diocese, came upon a funeral procession of exactly no one; the mortician was simply taking the body in a cart after the church service to the grave. The bishop got out of the car and followed on foot. We should not live alone, and we should not die alone. For a time we may wish to mourn alone, but the time after the funeral, especially the first year, is when friends count most and can do many helpful things.